Boys, Booze, and Bathroom Floors

Boys, Booze, and Bathroom Floors

Forty-Six Tales about the Collision of Suicide Grief and Dating

MICHELLE MILLER

Cover art by Paul Ribera
Cover graphic design by Jenny Jaramillo
ISBN: 1535510730
ISBN 13: 9781535510738
Library of Congress Control Number: 2016912313
CreateSpace Independent Publishing Platform
North Charleston, South Carolina

This book is affectionately dedicated to my eight-year-old self, who sat at her school desk one day and thought, "I want to be a writer."

This book is also dedicated to those who grieve and do so without eloquence or pretension.

Table of Contents

So I Don't
Get Sued

The following stories are true or based on true events. I have changed the names and identifying details of everyone in this book, especially my male costars, in order to protect their fragile little egos from being damaged and my fragile little bank account from being drained by lawsuits. It needs to be said that if lawsuits did not exist, I would expose them all.

The only names that have not been changed are those of my late husband and myself.

Oh, and to all my blond female readers—my references to you in this book are not an accurate reflection of my true feelings toward all women with golden strands. I was simply very jealous of blondes when I wrote this book. It was not just because of the blonde-versus-brunette cold war that has existed since the beginning of time, but because during the time frame in which this book was written, all the women that I got dumped for were in fact blond. I have since forgiven all of you for this genetic (and sometimes chemically altered) state.

An Introduction So Short, You Won't Be Tempted to Skip It

In January 2014 I was getting divorced. Again. I was thirty-one years old with two children, a mortgage, and a part-time job.

I began psychotherapy and a second job. I picked up two Bible studies, read one self-help book a week, and started dating for the first time in ten years.

A few months into the separation from my husband, he took his own life after penning a lengthy suicide note blaming me.

I quit psychotherapy and both my jobs. I renounced anything related to religion, vetoed all reading material by anyone with a PhD, and joined four online dating sites.

These are some of those dates.

Denial: dih-nahy-uh l (noun) Pretending your life doesn't completely suck.

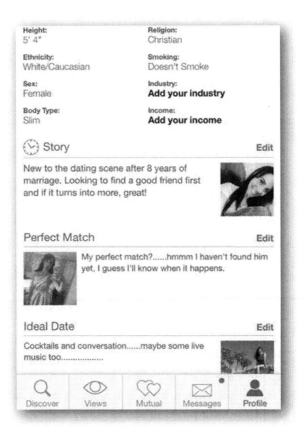

Height: 5' 4"	**Religion:** Christian
Ethnicity: White/Caucasian	**Smoking:** Doesn't Smoke
Sex: Female	**Industry:** **Add your industry**
Body Type: Slim	**Income:** **Add your income**

🕑 Story   Edit

New to the dating scene after 8 years of marriage. Looking to find a good friend first and if it turns into more, great!

Perfect Match   Edit

My perfect match?......hmmm I haven't found him yet, I guess I'll know when it happens.

Ideal Date   Edit

Cocktails and conversation......maybe some live music too.................

Discover   Views   Mutual   Messages   Profile

Date One: Chosen, Wanted, Desired

With a chronic case of just-been-fucked jet-black hair, muted green eyes, tattoo-covered muscles, and a six-foot-four body, Number One could be frightening if not for the way his smile transforms his face into a very young version of himself. He grew up parallel to me in this same small town in Southern California, but I always steered clear of him as stories of his huge penis and notorious partying intimidated me. He had joined the ranks of men who were out of my league when, the summer after my senior year in high school, his homemade porno tapes started surfacing at parties while I was still a virgin.

Then, seemingly out of nowhere, in his early twenties, Number One did something quite shocking: he got a wife, a nine-to-five job, and two daughters.

We meet for the first time on Valentine's Day, a few weeks after I left my marriage for good, while my best friend, Lynnette (who was going through a divorce of her own), and I are sharing sorrows and drinks at the local bowling alley.

Pause. A side note on my best friend, Lynnette.

To simply call her my "best friend" underplays the depth of the bond we have created over the last decade and a half. Yes, she is my best friend, but, more than that, at this time in my life, she became essential to my survival. She had no boundaries with me, nor I with her. She never judged. Never told me I went too far. Never said I was wrong for anything I felt, unspoken or not. She metaphorically planted her feet into the shaky earth that surrounded me and refused to retract her loyalty under any circumstance. She became the pillar I bounced off and around, and at the same time that she was my stability, she was also my partner in chaos. She bounced with me and stood beside me and carried me in her arms and hoisted me onto her back—all at once, even though this is physically impossible, and she lived three hours away.

When I was especially hard on myself for a drinking binge or a sex-with-multiple-men weekend, she'd stop me midsentence and say, "Michelle, you are a widow. A *widow*. Your husband is dead; give yourself a break." Sometimes I would. Sometimes I wouldn't. In both instances, she was there.

Okay, back to how I found myself on an accidental date with the former porn star turned dad…

Lynnette had talked me into buying a pair of matching black leather leggings and convinced me to wear them with her on a barhopping Valentine's Day adventure in an attempt to free ourselves from our "boring wife wardrobes." She said the leggings would be lucky.

The tequila hits my bloodstream just as the outline of Number One's large frame emerges from the black lights coming from the lanes of the bowling alley to our booth at the bar. Lynnette, who has never been intimidated by anything that has a penis, waves to him. As I turn to look, I decide instantly that I am not attracted to him, which I find odd because he is so very attractive. He sits across from us, and as the drinks keep coming, we all discuss with sarcasm the reality of the bar scene here in this small town. Lynnette, however, brags about the abundance of singles where she lives in San Diego.

While waiting for our cocktails to arrive, the three of us break down the small-town dating scene into three categories: the young military guys with wedding-band tan lines who are only looking to get laid; the dreaded gym-rat meathead types who live at home with their moms; and the broke divorcés who have to charge their drinks on credit cards.

"That's me!" Number One says.

"You're getting divorced?" I say in surprise. "Me too!" And we clink the glasses of our newly arrived cocktails before finishing the drinks in less than three gulps.

Alcohol makes the rest of this night blurry, but I remember at one point deciding to go to a house party. Or maybe Lynnette decided this for me—being a thirty-one-year-old at a house party doesn't seem like something I would choose to do on my own.

When we pull up to the curb, Number One opens the door and offers his hand to help me out of the elevated truck. My fingers touch his palm, and I instantly have the feeling of falling, or is it spinning? There is some sort of disconnect between my brain and stilettos, which is just an eloquent way of saying I am drunker than I thought.

Number One lets me fall into him, into his chest. He is ridiculously stable, like he has been anticipating and maybe even looking forward to catching me when, not if, I fall. I look up, seeking out his facial features to find them blacked out, and the circumference of his face illuminated from the streetlamp behind him. What a shame; I really want to see his eyes. As I search his shadowed face, sensations dormant in me for so long that I have forgotten they even exist begin to descend upon me in waves.

The first sensation is the unrestrained, magnetic pull of a boy's lips to mine as Number One kisses me. It's my first kiss from anyone other than my husband in ten years. This is followed by the cold February chill dissipating with the warmth of our torsos becoming indistinguishable, leading into the best sensation of them all—relief. It is the relief of the weight of rejection, a weight I didn't even realize I was carrying. Relief—the very opposite of what my husband's multiple infidelities had made me feel.

Number One's kiss reminds me of the weightlessness of being chosen, wanted, and desired. Number One's kiss reminds me that I am alive.

The kiss was *that* good.

I guess these black leather leggings really are lucky. When Lynnette asks me later if it felt weird kissing someone new, I say, "Not at all. I feel like I have been divorced for years" because, in my heart, I had been.

Date Two: Crotches Devoid of Pubic Hair

I am not a fan of chain Italian-food restaurants. My grandmother was from Sicily, for goodness' sake! Formally frozen entrées reheated and masquerading as authentic Italian food annoy me, as does my date. It's been less than five minutes, four of which he's spent talking about his truck. I need a drink.

"Would you like to start out with a cocktail?" the plump, peppy waitress asks.

"Just iced tea for us both," Number Two says before I have a chance to open my mouth. "I'm in AA; ninety-two days sober," he says with pride. This will be our first, last, and only date, I decide right then and there.

Good thing I have a flask of vodka in my purse. I excuse myself to use the bathroom.

"I thought people in AA can't date for a year," I say, not even attempting to mask my accusatory tone when I return from my restroom chug session.

"Well, yeah, but this isn't really a date. We're just friends, right?"

"So you're not paying?"

"I'll still pay, as long as I'm getting at least a kiss at the end of the night," he says and then laughs uneasily when he sees I'm not amused.

"Sure thing!" I say with a smile. "I always kiss my 'just friends.'" He relaxes. He didn't pick up on my sarcasm. Idiot. I don't know this yet, but mixed signals and confusion about who pays the bill will not be an isolated dating incident.

Tonight will be the beginning of my rude awakening into a new type of dating world—a world so very different than when I last navigated successfully through it in 2004. It's 2014, and I will soon learn that the dating world is full of gray areas instead of black-and-white clarity. There are men who only pay to obligate a woman, instead of paying directly for the pleasure of her company. There are hookups instead of good-night kisses and fuck buddies instead of boyfriends. There is texting instead of talking, ghosting instead of breakups, dating apps and Facebook profiles instead of get-to-know-you conversations, dick pics instead of blind dates, and crotches devoid of pubic hair instead of, well, crotches that are not devoid of pubic hair.

I scan the menu for the most expensive entrée. I order the veal parmigiana and, later, two desserts.

When Number Two leans in to kiss me that night in the parking lot, I pull away and add an extra layer of degradation by shaking his hand.

I'll never go out with this kind of guy again.

Date Three: Patch of Chest Hair

I don't blame the wine, nor do I blame the lucky leather leggings (although they were both involved). I had sex with Number Three on purpose. I needed to get the feel of my husband erased. I needed to move on, or I'd go back to him. I needed to know what sex felt like with someone else. I needed to understand the feelings that provoked my husband to seek out the bodies of other women over the years. I needed a lot of things. Tonight I got them and more.

Sex with Number Three is sensual and unnervingly natural.

In the middle of the night, I wake up with my arm across his chest. I graze the surface of it with my hand, searching for that familiar patch of chest hair, until I realize he isn't my husband. Number Three has a smooth chest. I stop grazing, roll over to my back, and stare at the ceiling. I feel misplaced.

In nine days my husband will be dead.

Date Four: A Choice My Husband Did Not Make

We are driving down the Pacific Coast Highway, windows rolled down, hot sun on my skin, and the line of my mouth somewhere between a smile and a frown. It has been two weeks since my husband's death. "You're gonna love this place!" Number Four vows over the wind. At the next stop sign I look over to see a couple getting married on the beach, the bride in a blinding, pure-white ball gown and the groom in a classic tuxedo.

So inappropriate for a beach wedding, I think to myself. But then again, I married a man who was late to our wedding because he was sexting another woman and then showed up at the ceremony in Vans sneakers with no shoelaces and knock-off Oakley sunglasses. So what the fuck do I know?

"Aw! Will you look at that happy couple?" I squeal with overly enthusiastic sarcastic delight as I look out the window. Number Four lets out a chuckle; he always gets my sarcasm. "It's all fun and games until someone cheats on you, then offs himself," I say flatly. He drives on.

When we park, the nostalgic smell of marijuana overpowers the salty smell of the ocean. The view from the front seat of his car, as cliché as it sounds, is picturesque. I don't want to move. For the first time in weeks, I am comfortable. I am warm. I am hundreds of miles from the small town that will now only identify me as the "suicide widow." I just want to stare at the vastness of the water in the distance and pretend to be someone else.

I want this view of the ocean to invigorate me like it did when I was little. I want it to seduce me like it did when I was a teenager. I want it to mesmerize me like it did the first time I saw it through the eyes of my children. It does none of these things. I feel nothing but external warmth.

"It's kind of a hike," Number Four interrupts. He offers me his hand to help me out of the car, and to my surprise he doesn't let go even when I steady myself. Interlacing his foreign fingers in mine, Number Four guides me through the shrubs, pot smokers, trees, hippies, and half-clothed lovers until we get to the cliff that he promises he's never shown to anyone. I can't help but compare his hands to my husband's.

They are the first new hands I've held in ten years, and I don't know how to describe them, so I won't.

In the months and years following this day, I will be in countless physically intimate positions with dozens of men. They will take me to expensive restaurants, fast-food drive-thrus, dive bars, karaoke bars, penthouses, and parking lots. They will buy me things, introduce me to their families, and ask me to babysit their dogs. They will tell me they love me, they hate me, they want to save me, or they want to fuck me. They will hold my purse, my car door open, and my hair back when I'm throwing up that sixth shot of tequila, but no one other than Number Four will ever hold my hand.

When we arrive, Number Four lays down a blanket a few feet from a ledge. We stare in silence at the water as he opens a beer. To describe the view in front of me with mere words would be an injustice, so I won't.

This day is not about romance. We don't kiss, have sex, or have any profound conversations. We just sit there—sometimes silent and sometimes discussing mutual childhood friends, our dissatisfaction with work, and the lyrical genius of Stevie Nicks's "Landslide." Number Four is comfort; he always has been, ever since we were kids.

There is a moment between sips of beer and verbalizing my thoughts on Number Four's uncle's Jack Russell terrier when I realize how close I am to falling to my death on the rocks and water below. In an instant, I think of how my own death would mean avoiding the observation of my children's lifelong grief. I think of how my death would mean avoiding the fingers continuing to point at me when I return home tomorrow. I think of how my death would mean avoiding the what-ifs, the guilt. I think of how my death would mean never having to face the fact that I'll never really be in love or receive love freely again.

I take a sip of beer.

"You can have the rest," Number Four offers.

"Nah, I don't like beer." I stand up and peer over the ledge. "Do you think anyone's ever died up here?"

"I guess it's a possibility," he says in his easy, casual tone while lying on his back, half propped up by his elbows.

As I look down at the massive boulders and the water crashing on them, I think of how my death would mean avoiding the observation of my children's victory over trauma. I think of how my death would mean avoiding pointing my middle finger at the assholes who think I'm to blame for my husband's suicide. I think of how my death would mean avoiding the epiphanies, the lessons, and the ability to relate to others who have also been broken. I think of how my death would mean never having to face the fact that I can live a good life without ever experiencing romantic love again because I am enough.

It feels too soon for acceptance, but acceptance shows up anyway and reminds me I am not in control of my grief time line. For a few hours on the cliff, I accept this life I did not ask for. I make the decision to live for my kids, for myself, for the friends I haven't even met yet, and for the hope of a sale on my favorite mascara and the guarantee of delight that tacos and margaritas with Lynnette will bring.

I will be fine. I will make it out of this. The worst of my grief is over. I will hold on to the memory of looking down over the edge and out at the sea and the consistency in the tone of Number Four's voice over the rhythm of the waves. I will choose life over death every day—a choice my husband did not make.

Date Five: Talk about a Threesome!

I am playing footsie under the long white cloth of my table with Number Five or his friend—I'm not sure which. It doesn't matter, though, since they are both buying me shots. They are the epitome of the male-bimbo twentysomething gym-rat duo, and they chose to sit across from my friends and me at this year's annual Kick Cancer benefit.

Three shots later, Number Five grabs my leg, removes my gold wedge heel, and puts my foot on the huge bulge between his legs. This is while we are politely chatting with the oblivious, elderly man at our table who lost his wife to cancer.

I am in over my head.

Not only is Number Five way out of my league physically, but also, I have never done anything like this and I can tell that he has. It doesn't really matter, though, because the whiskey I've been ingesting all night is telling me that sex with Number Five is my destiny.

As the evening begins to die down, and our table empties, Number Five licks his lips, leans in toward me, and says, "So, what are we gonna do?"

I lean in, make unwavering eye contact, and say, "I don't want a relationship, but I don't want a one-night stand either. What I need is a long-term fuck buddy. My husband shot and killed himself a few weeks ago after cheating on me for our entire marriage, and I have zero tolerance for bullshit, especially from you men."

"Meet me in the parking lot in five minutes," Number Five says. I do so, in part because I am completely in love with the fact that he had no reaction to the "my husband shot and killed himself" statement. All the other people in this town either ignore me for their own comfort or treat me like a mental patient, which is also for their own comfort.

Four minutes and fifty-nine seconds later, I am in the front seat of Number Five's car with his right hand up my dress. We drive to his house but don't even make it inside, mainly because his mother is there, and that would be awkward because she was in one of the Bible studies I used to attend.

(For the record, Number Five is over the age of eighteen, but only barely.)

The sex is hot and rough and dirty. It's when I climb on top of Number Five in the passenger seat that my husband shows up. Not physically, of course, because he is dead, but he's there nonetheless. Number Five's hands are roaming purposefully over every inch of my body. They are alternately my husband's scarred, calloused blue-collar work hands and Number Five's smoother, slightly callused weight-lifting hands.

Talk about a threesome!

Luckily the whiskey overcomes the tears that begin to well up. I enjoy myself, even though I have to fake an orgasm—although Number Five is gifted on a technical level, he doesn't make me feel as sexy as Number Four did last night.

Is my husband going to show up every time I have sex? I contemplated this question the next morning while finding solace in the cold off-white tile of the bathroom floor. Thirty minutes and three vomits later, I came to the conclusion that the only way to find out is to keep having sex with hot younger men.

My husband controlled my life when he was alive, and I'll be damned if he's going to control my life when he's dead. I refuse to give him the satisfaction of turning me into a celibate spinster—because being an underweight, reckless binge drinker is much better.

Date Six: My Vagina Is Worth Forty-Five Dollars

Number Six and I decide to finally meet up in a hotel room in a city that is halfway between us, after chatting through the Plenty of Fish dating app for the last month. When I arrive, I realize it is a motel, not a hotel, and that he has chosen one with a marquee that reads, "$45 and a Free Continental Breakfast."

My vagina is worth forty-five dollars...and a free continental breakfast, should I choose to stay until morning. I won't stay until morning. I can't risk a man witnessing one of my night terrors.

Fastening my khaki-colored trench coat over my black corset, G-string, and fishnet thigh-high stockings, I slide my feet into my red stilettos and play the part. Once Number Six sees what's under my trench coat, he doesn't last long. After an hour of chitchat about who the hottest member of the *Saved by the Bell* cast was, we go at it again. I know I won't finish; the stale aroma of the red industrial carpet and my apathy overwhelms any sensations I have in my genitals. I fake it. He doesn't.

When I get home that night, after I relieve the babysitter, I stand in the hallway between the open doors of my children's bedrooms. I feel nothing. The memory of what it had once been like to ache with love as I watched my son and daughter sleep is fleeting and draining. I will never be able to experience tenderness again, I decide. I make my way to the liquor cabinet.

Once in my bedroom, I strip off my sex clothes and lie naked diagonally on my king-size bed. Thoughts of my husband flash through my mind with each rotation of the ceiling fan—the skin on his knuckles, the place where his hairline faded into his neck, the coarse hair surrounding his nipples. I sip the Bacardi 151 and pretend that Number Six loves me and I'm not just a hole for his dick, until I sleep.

Date Seven: She's Happy Her Husband's Dead

She said that...Michelle, I really don't want to tell you what she said." Number Seven looks down into the dark burgundy of his wineglass.

"Tell me. I'd rather know what people are saying behind my back," I assert.

"She just said that...you know...she just pointed out that you and your husband were separated when he died."

I can tell there is more that he's not telling me. I raise my right eyebrow. "And?" I say, challenging him. I know this is a heavy conversation, even for a sixth date, but I still press him for answers. I need the pain. I need the hatred to continue its feast on me. I need to be skinned and filleted. Eaten and digested. Expelled. I need to be the victim.

"And just that you don't really seem that sad because, on Facebook, you're out all the time partying and taking pictures in new clothes," Number Seven continues cautiously.

"Tell me her exact words." I say through gritted teeth.

"Are you sure?"

"Yes," I say.

"Okay, then." He gets a serious look on his face. "She said, 'She's happy her husband's dead because they were getting divorced anyway,' but she wasn't trying to be mean or anything. She just seemed confused about why you seem so happy, 'cause widows are usually not."

The pain of being judged is a unique ailment because it happens inside of your core. It makes you question who you know yourself to be.

She's right, I decide. I do seem happy on Facebook. And it would be a lie to say that there aren't parts of me that are indeed happy. Maybe "happy" is the wrong word. Relieved? I had been so afraid of my husband when we separated. I'd get late-night texts and calls with him yelling, slurring, and cursing at me. Sometimes, after a night out, I'd pull into the driveway of my parents' house, where the kids and I had moved, to find him standing down the street, staring at me with a shovel in his hand, laughing while I ran inside.

Not to mention the fears I had surrounding the divorce. He only saw the kids twice during the two months before his death, even though the kids and I were next door at my parents'. Despite his lack of interest in the kids, though, I had a feeling that once the divorce paperwork started, he'd fight me for custody just out of spite.

Was I happy he was dead? No. Was I relieved? Yes—and this only added an extra layer to my already stifling guilt.

I ask Number Seven to refill my wineglass. He obliges. When we have sex for the first time that night, I cry afterward, and he makes fun of me. The familiarity of this type of pain is comforting.

Date Eight: Little Gold Dress and Flesh-Colored G-String

I just got dumped by two men within thirty minutes. One of them was going on a weekend getaway with one of his many girlfriends, and the other decided to go back to his needy ex-girlfriend.

To make matters worse, my designated driver and gay boyfriend backed out of our date to the hospital fundraiser dinner tonight so he could spend time with his mom.

Talk about your gay-man stereotype.

I am alone at a table of relative strangers in an amazing gold dress that none of my boyfriends will be able to fully appreciate now. The only way to salvage this evening is to keep drinking margaritas and post pictures of myself on that little social-media foreplay center called Facebook.

Within thirty-two seconds of posting my first picture, I get a text from Number Eight.

I fucking love Facebook.

He tells me I look great in my dress and that if I need anything tonight, he is available. Hmm, *do* I need anything? Why yes! Yes, I do. I'll need a ride home after I finish off my fifth margarita.

But—*gasp*! Oh no! The only vehicle Number Eight has tonight is his Harley, and I am in a dress. Whatever shall we do?

Number Eight pulls up fifteen minutes later and hands me a helmet and jacket. The small audience that began to form when he pulled up to the venue is now getting an eyeful as I straddle the seat of the motorcycle in my amazing little gold dress and flesh colored G-string.

Just when this town was running out of interesting things about me to gossip about, I get drunk and straddle Number Eight just in time for everyone to discuss it at church the next morning.

You're welcome, little town!

And thank *you* because now my little gold dress is getting the attention it so rightly deserves, even if it's not from my boyfriends.

"Where are we going?" Number Eight yells over the vibration of the engine.

"Anywhere!" I scream. "Just take me now!" And so he does.

Sometimes I wish my life were a reality show, so I could have seen video of the looks on people's faces that night as we peeled out of the parking lot, my gold dress flapping in the breeze.

As we approach Main Street, I am pressed up close enough to Number Eight to keep my dress from flying up in the front, but I have no idea what's going on in the back. I'm pretty sure I flash my ass to half the town, but I don't care—I'm free.

Or drunk. These days, it's kind of hard to tell.

Either way, there is something to be said about the freedom one experiences when living though a horrible tragedy such as infidelity and subsequent suicide. It is similar to the feeling of riding down Main Street, going well above the speed limit, the breeze blowing up your dress without inhibition, in the middle of the night.

I have no control. *You* have no control. Once you realize this fact, you are freed from the task of lording over your life and the lives of others.

It is liberating to realize that motorcycles roll and kill people instantly and that husbands cheat and lie.

Terrorists set off bombs.

Children drown or get kidnapped.

And a soon-to-be-ex-husband texts you a suicide note and takes a twelve-gauge shotgun out into the desert and pulls the trigger while you are on the phone with him, begging him to drop the gun.

And you are left to clean up the emotional mess of the children he has victimized, and they too must realize, at the tender ages of eleven and seven, that they have no control over the actions of others.

None.

Zero.

On the back of that motorcycle, tears stream down my face as thoughts of control and freedom come to my mind, and I can't keep from screaming obscenities and grinning from ear to ear beneath the hard plastic face shield of my motorcycle helmet. Number Eight probably thinks I'm a lunatic, because I am, but I couldn't care less.

I hold tighter as I sob tears of joy that roll onto my exposed neck and onto his black leather jacket. I am sixteen again and ditching third-period French class to go joyriding in my crush's '68 Mustang. I am nine years old at summer camp, on the lake with my best friend, singing at the top of my lungs. I am free as fuck and have been given a new perspective on life.

Or I am drunk. Maybe drunk people see things that sober people aren't brave enough to.

When Number Eight brings me home and helps me off with my helmet, I aggressively kiss him, only to find that he returns my forcefulness with a soft slowness. I am taken aback and hastily pull myself off him. He puts his hand around my waist and pulls me gently to him, and we share an amazing kiss just before the rain starts to fall.

Cue background music.

Yet another reason I should have my own reality show.

I pull away as the kiss gets more emotional, still surprised at Number Eight's tenderness, and stumble inside. The next morning, I realize I have a second-degree burn on my leg from the motorcycle's exhaust, but I don't mind.

I hope the burn permanently scars me so that even when I am old, I can be reminded of the breeze going up my dress that night and the bonds of control that were broken by my husband's suicide.

Date Nine: Inhale

It feels wrong discussing Christianity while naked in the backseat of a car with Number Nine. It also feels wrong that Number Nine has a Bible verse tattooed on his forearm. He is the very opposite of anything Christian. I am tracing the words from the Holy Scriptures with my pinky finger while my head rests in his lap. He is methodically stroking my hair. I begin to mouth, "And we know that in all things, God works for the good of those…"

He joins me in repeating the last part aloud: "Who love Him and who have been called according to His purpose."

"Romans 8:28," he says. "I gotta get that shit covered soon." He clears his throat.

"That shit?" I ask.

"Yeah. Shit." He inhales from the pipe.

"You're not a believer anymore?"

"Fuck, no," he says, exhaling. "That piece-of-shit book did nothing for me when my son died. All those years of Sunday school and vacation Bible school and fucking church camp, and…just, nothing helped." Silence for several minutes. "Why? Are you a Christian or something?"

"No," I admit for the first time to anyone. The word leaves my lips so naturally—no. "Was it scary to give up God?" I unintentionally wonder aloud.

"Scary?" He laughs.

"Yeah. Was it, like, scary to give up something like that, that you had believed in your whole life?"

"No," he says in confusion. "It was a relief." He offers me the pipe, and I inhale.

Date Ten: Lines of Cocaine on Her Breasts

Number Ten and I stumble into the blinding white light of the living room from his master bedroom at two o'clock in the morning. There is an insanely beautiful woman, no older than twenty-two, lying naked on a yard-sale-quality coffee table with lines of cocaine on her breasts and abs. The carpet is shit brown and sculpted. Her hair is platinum blond. She is makeup-free except for her false eyelashes. She is tanned and devoid of body hair. She is surrounded by men.

"Do you want to do some coke?" Number Ten asks.

"No thanks," I say, trying to hide my discomfort.

"Sorry. Just didn't know if you were into that or not. I don't do it either—it makes me uncomfortable."

Number Ten offers to take me back to my vehicle, which I left at the bar. I let him.

As I walk past her, I think about how other people live their twenties so differently than I did. I think about how the naked woman being used as a platter for drugs and lust is not that different from me. I think about how full of power that woman is, even though she is motionless. I think about how different my birthday is this year than last, when I got handmade construction-paper cards from the kids and oral sex in the shower from my husband.

Date Eleven: Seven Minutes

My hair smells like cigarette smoke and bad decisions from the night before. The cemetery smells like fresh-cut grass and stillness from the recent rainstorm. I wake up in the afternoon heat, crying on his grave. Grass clippings are embedded in my face, and ants crawl on my bare feet. It would've been our nine-year wedding anniversary today.

I will never grow old with him. I will never grow old with anyone. This will kill me.

I get the sudden urge to go out to the spot in the desert where my husband perished. The spot where he changed the course of my and the kids' lives.

I trudge through the grainy sand and creosote bushes in my flip-flops. My eyes fixate on the heat ripples rising from the earth that create a path away from civilization. Instantly, I am sweating and thirsty, but I just keep walking west until I can no longer hear noise from the cars on Irwin Road.

When I reach the boulders where my husband and I used to take the kids for shooting practice, I turn and head south a few hundred feet. When I am satisfied at my estimation of where he took his last breath, I stop, take my eyes off the waves of hot air that had guided me out here, and take notice of my surroundings. In front of me, to the south, is the small desert town I grew up in.

It appears so very tiny and overly sheltered by mountain ranges on each side. It had never occurred to me until this moment that I lived in a valley.

I guess we really don't know the things surrounding us until we are outside of them.

To the west, east, and north of me is nothing but sky and uneven beige landscapes peppered with the occasional splash of other, more pleasing earth tones. The silence is more intense than the heat and second only to the feeling of loneliness. The feeling of aloneness is palpable. It is like one of those dreams I had as a child of being the last person on the planet while wandering the streets looking for my brother. How much more intense must that feeling of loneliness have been for my husband in the dark as he lay on his back waiting for death to come?

Seven minutes.

Seven minutes is how long the coroner estimated it took for my husband to bleed out. I lie down cautiously, allowing my skin to acclimate to the scorching sand, and set the timer on my phone for seven minutes. I decide for that length of time, and that length of time only, I will not hate him. I will empathize with him, because although hating him gives me energy, it gives me exhaustion as well, and I need respite from this hatred-induced fatigue that I feel in my bones every second of every day.

Hating him has also been a great barrier preventing me from missing him and the most effective coping mechanism for my depression at this point. As I lie down, I am nervous, but remind myself I will readopt my hatred for him after this seven-minute hiatus.

I don't know if it's tears, sweat, or the blinding cloudless sky, but my eyes burn immediately. I close them and focus on breathing as I let my mind imagine his last seven minutes on earth.

What was the last thing his eyes saw?

What was the last sound his ears heard?

Was he thirsty?

Did he regret his choice?

Did his life flash before his eyes as the old cliché goes? Was I part of that flash?

Did he decide to believe in God?

Was he happy that he had gotten his revenge on me for leaving him?

Did he wonder who would take our daughter on her field trip next week in his absence?

Did he think about the shape our son's eyes would morph into when I told him that his dad was dead?

Did he feel guilty for doing this to his father? His sister? His mother? *His mother.*

Did he wonder what our kids would tell their kids about him?

Was he excited that his existence was about to be over?

Was he so blinded by pain and selfishness that he couldn't even think of these things?

When the timer goes off, I don't move. I lie there and cry for several minutes, tears mixing with my sweat and creating mud underneath my head, and all the while, I am choosing not to miss my anger, choosing not to hold on to my guilt. I simply empathize with him. I think of his body and what a bullet in it must've felt like. This is easier to comprehend than his mental state.

I cannot fathom his despair. Even when I think of my own despair, I know my suffering is miniscule compared to his in the moments before his death.

Burning.

Fire.

Stinging.

Expanding.

Rupturing.

Bleeding.

The bleeding.

The massive bleeding.

I think of how I always took care of my husband's physical ailments with Band-Aids and ointments and gauze and sometimes emergency-room visits. I think of how strong my urge to nurture him always was. I think of how these last few years I wanted so badly to fix his brain, to make him be the man I thought he was. The man he pretended to be but at the end of it all, never was.

I spend the rest of the day in bed. No shower, no change of clothes. I spend the rest of the day feeling the unsavory feelings I'd kept at bay for so long. Empathy, longing, and sorrow. I spend the rest of the day sober.

Until Number Eleven facebook messages me.

Eighteen hours later, I wake up naked in a strange living room. I wish I don't know the man lying next to me, but I do. I wish I hadn't crossed that line, but I did.

31

"Where are you going?" Number Eleven's raspy voice whispers as I search for my clothes.

"I gotta go. This never happened. Don't tell anyone, okay?" The room is spinning, and I curse as I step on an empty shot glass.

"Can I get your number?" he asks while laughing at my lack of coordination.

"Did you hear what I just said?" I scold as I pull my clothes from between the couch cushions and hastily apply them to my emaciated body. "This *never* happened, I was *never* here, and we will *never* speak of this again." I frantically try to get dressed, but the pounding in my head is making it difficult.

"Oh, come on, Michelle!" he says as he sits up and wraps himself in a blanket. "Because of the Rachel thing? We broke up, like, six months ago, and we weren't even serious or anything." A good point, but still unconvincing. And is he going to mention the fact that he was friends with my husband, or are we both going to pretend that he wasn't some sort of twisted revenge fuck for me?

"It is an unwritten rule that you don't hook up with a friend's ex, and Rachel is my friend. You men have the same rule, and you know it!" He can't argue. What we did was wrong.

The worst part of all of this is not the fact that I hurt Rachel. It's not the fact that our friendship will never be the same when, a few days later, I confess to her what I did, and it's not even the fact that I'm about to do the walk of shame in front of Number Eleven's neighbors. No, the absolute worst part of all of this is that given the chance, I would do it all again.

I am that selfish.

And broken.

And self-entitled.

And lonely.

And angry.

And depressed.

The emotional payoff from conquering Number Eleven at the expense of my health, my friendships, and time with my kids is *that* strong of a reward for me. Sex gives me and outlet for my rage, erases my guilt, and the lingering insecurities caused by my husband's infidelities, even if the sex only lasts between two minutes (really, Number Five?) and two hours (I miss Number Four—maybe I will get back together with him again). During those minutes or hours, I am not being increasingly strangled by the weight my husband placed inside of my ribcage with his death, and I will sacrifice anything for this momentary relief.

I will sacrifice *anything*, and I will sacrifice everything too.

I have this revelation on my bathroom floor, an hour after I leave Number Eleven's house and my hangover really kicks in. Suddenly I'm caught off guard by sympathy for the other women who helped destroy my marriage. If I slept with one of my friend's exes, how far am I from sleeping with a married man? I'll bet all of my husband's whores started out this way.

Empathy begins to overwhelm me until it is surpassed by guilt about the fact that I am the reason my husband is dead. Why couldn't I just forgive him? Why didn't I just stay with him? Why couldn't I see that the force behind his pursuit of other women for all those years was because of his own brokenness, not my lackluster? How could I have not looked past my own pain about his cheating to see that he was drowning all those years? What the fuck was he so broken over?

I'll never know now. Never. He is not here for us to have that conversation.

My victim mentality had been telling me I was the helpless wife of a selfish man. He broke his wedding vows of fidelity, but what about my vows? What about "in sickness and in health"? I failed at my vows as much as he did at his. I refused him the forgiveness he needed, and I forsook him in sickness and only wanted to stay with him in good mental health.

Had I taken a minute to come down from my high horse during the last few years of my marriage and admitted to myself and to my husband that I too was imperfect, he'd still be alive.

I drove him to suicide.

This entire thing is my fault.

My fault.

I should've spent my anniversary watching our wedding video and crying like normal widows do, instead of going to that bar in my black leather leggings with Number Eleven. Curse the black leather leggings!

I can't do this anymore. I cannot exist here in this little town surrounded by people who used to know my husband. I cannot exist here in this little town surrounded by people who used to know me.

I am not me anymore.

And so, a month later, the kids and I are living in San Diego with Lynnette and her three kids. Moving will fix everything.

Bargaining: bahr-guh n ing (verb) Thinking you have control over your life.

Michelle, 32
less than a mile away Active just now

5'4 120lbs....hate exercise, love bacon and chocolate so I will probably be fat one day, but for now my metabolism is awesome. Outgoing introvert, widowed after 8 years of marriage, unemployed but financially independent, 2 children that you won't be meeting anytime soon, recently moved to ███████ and looking for someone to explore the area with when my kids are visiting their grandparents on weekends. No, I will not send you nude pics, and I am morally opposed to cleavage selfies.

Date Twelve: Like Virgins

I will do it right. I will make him wait for sex.

It is the fourth date before I even let Number Twelve kiss me, and it is worth the wait. After a decadent five-course French meal in downtown San Diego, followed by front-row seats and a meet and greet with a nationally renowned magician, we are walking hand in hand through a park by Old Town. I can't see the stars or the moon, but I can feel them watching us and saying to each other, "Those two have potential. How lucky we are to be witnessing the beginning of something so beautiful."

I squeal as the breeze blows up my maroon handkerchief halter dress, causing the hemline to achieve such heights that it threatens to reveal I'm not wearing underwear. I am Marilyn Monroe, pushing my dress down and giggling. He, being the gentleman I know him to be, does not let his eyes wander to my exposed skin and instead offers me his jacket. As he drapes his black suit jacket over my shoulders, he allows both his hands to move down the length of my arms until he reaches my hands.

I make eye contact to give him permission to kiss me. And kiss me, he does! With our fingers interlaced, he slowly navigates the unknown terrain of my lips, and then he explores my cheeks and earlobes. When he reaches my neck, the fireworks start, literally—fireworks from Sea World start going off, as if to match our arousal level.

Purple. Glisten. Sizzle. Gold. White. Sparkle. Heat. Explosion.

I want to have sex with him right then and there, standing in the grass, but I won't. I will do this the right way. I will make him wait.

He pulls away briefly, and we both laugh. "Talk about perfect timing," he says. And we kiss more. And then some more. We kiss, and we kiss, and we kiss. We kiss like teenagers who just learned how to kiss and who can't get over the novelty. We kiss like virgins who have decided to stay virgins and who are now forced to express with only the act of kissing how very much we mean to each other. We kiss, and only kiss, until the late hours of the night.

The next morning my lips are chapped and I'm smiling. I'm so glad I stopped at kissing. I'm so glad I'm making him wait for sex. If I wasn't being restrained by all the covers and pillows on my bed right now, I'd pat myself on the back for this major advancement in my hormonal resistance. What a mature woman I am turning into! Number Twelve and I, we have potential. This really is the beginning of something special. It's so nice to know that I am desired and respected. When we do finally have sex, it will be amazing.

I leisurely begin to check all my usual social-media updates. Sunday morning is my favorite time to do this because I get to peer into everyone's Saturday night. Snapchat is my favorite of these apps; all of the pictures and videos are live and lack inhibition because both the pictures and video clips disappear forever after ten seconds. At the top of my incoming snap list is a snap video from Number Twelve. It was sent at 3:45 a.m. He must have been up late after our date, thinking of me!

I eagerly press the purple button to reveal the video. Number Twelve is with a group of friends, obviously drunk. I guess he needed to go out and blow off some steam once our date was over. Good for him.

I keep watching as the last three seconds of the video show Number Twelve grabbing a beautiful blond woman, dipping her at her waist, and kissing her aggressively on the mouth.

I text him:

Me: Good morning! I see you went out after our date last night.

Number Twelve: Yeah! We got so hammered.

Me: Yes, I noticed that. Listen, Number Twelve, I really like you and thought we had potential. Looking at last night's snap, it seems you are still in the "party and date lots of women" stage of your life, and I am in the "settle down and date one person" stage. If you ever want to seriously date me, give me a call. Until then, good luck to you and the blonde.

Number Twelve: LOL LOL hahahahaha! That woman was my friend's wife!

Date Thirteen: Mr. Good-Choice Boyfriend

I will do it right. I will make him wait for sex.

Number Thirteen will be a "good choice" boyfriend. Who says you can't meet a decent man on the Zoosk dating app? He is clean-cut, has a steady job, has never been married, has no kids, is Christian, and comes from a nice upper-middle-class family from the San Diego suburbs.

On our second date, after a movie, he invites me out to a karaoke bar where he is meeting with friends. I decline because I am going to do this right! I am going to make him wait for sex, and karaoke is like the black leather leggings for me. I don't know why bad singing is an aphrodisiac, but it is—don't judge. He walks me to my car and kisses me good night after asking when he can see me again. We decide on dinner next weekend.

The next morning, I wake up to a live Snapchat video from him. It was sent at 1:00 a.m. I am hesitant to open it. What if it is like Number Twelve's video and he's kissing some woman? It can't be that bad. It's probably just a video of him singing karaoke after a few too many beers.

I press the purple button.

Porn. Why is Number Thirteen sending me a video clip of the blow-job porn he is watching? Crippled by my shock, I can't look away. I continue watching and notice the caption on the video reads, "This could be you," with a red arrow pointing at the blond woman bobbing her head up and down. Blond—they are always fucking blond! Before I even have a chance to process my disgust, the camera moves from the woman, up a man's torso, and onto a face—Number Thirteen's face. It wasn't porn after all. It was a live video of Number Thirteen, Mr. Potential. Mr. Good-Choice Boyfriend was getting head.

Date Fourteen: A Deranged Horny Frog

I will do it right. I will make him wait for sex.

I should've known the sex would be bad. I should have got it out of the way on the first damn date. On our third date, when he kisses me, his small, pointy tongue darts in and out of my mouth like a deranged horny frog. His penis is the same.

We are on a sailboat drifting off into the sunset, for fuck's sake; this is supposed to be slow and romantic, damn it! But it's not. It's quick and sharp and dry.

"That was so great, baby," he whispers breathlessly in my ear while lying on top of my stiff body. "You feel so good."

How am I going to get out of this one? If I only knew how to drive this boat, I could toss him overboard and head back to the dock!

"I'm so lucky to have found you," he continues, still high on endorphins or dopamine or whatever the hell chemicals men's brains release when they cum in less than three minutes. "How is it that you're still single?"

And then I know how I will get rid of Number Fourteen. Finally, after so many times being rejected after (and sometimes during) a date, I know the exact thing to say to make men run away.

"Well, I'm not technically single. I'm widowed. My husband shot and killed himself a year ago, leaving behind me and my kids."

"I'm sorry to hear that," he says after a long pause. "I didn't know you had kids." He starts getting dressed.

I don't hear from him until four days later, when he texts me and says he's too busy with work to pursue any kind of romantic relationship with me. Not all men are scared off by my kids. Not all men are scared off by my suicide-widow status. But all men everywhere are scared off by the combination of the two.

Date Fifteen: The Male Ego Is That Grand

I will do it right. I will make him wait for sex.

First date: cocktails and appetizers after matching on the Bumble dating app. We have so much in common.

Second date: the beach. We both look good in a bathing suit.

Third date: a movie. Our kissing tells me we will be sexually compatible.

Fourth date: we are in Number Fifteen's living room in the middle of the day, sober, watching Diane Lane in *Unfaithful*. Of course we are going to have sex now—we've just watched Diane Lane get taken from behind while she curses in pleasure!

So you can understand my shock when, after the combination of Diane Lane mostly naked and me topless kissing his neck, his penis is just lying there like a wet noodle when I unzip his pants. And it remains that way for an hour despite my efforts. Actually, his limp dick probably lasted for more than an hour, but I used the "I gotta go check on the kids" excuse to get the hell out of there.

I feel so bad for him that I spend the next three days in a row calling and texting him more than usual to reassure him that I still like him, re-assure him that he is still a man. I compliment him, stroke his ego, and completely avoid the wet-noodle topic. Maybe he was just nervous. We will try again when I see him on Saturday night.

Friday night, Lynnette and I go out for drinks and a stalking session directed at the new bartender she is crushing on. While she occupies herself with the bearded bartender, and the bearded bartender occupies himself with her cleavage, I scan the barstools for our competition (I always scope out the women at bars first, then the men). I see a plain-looking blond woman at the east side of the bar with her back to me. She will be our greatest competition tonight (the blondes usually are), so I must befriend her.

I instantly regret sitting next to her. She is obviously on a date with the man to her left, I have wasted my time, she isn't a threat, and I have lost my previous seat at the bar to one of those creepy Rico Suave–looking guys with the perfect stubble and a lisp.

I also regret the amount of time it took me to notice that the blond woman's date is in fact Mr. Noodle himself, Number Fifteen. Number Fifteen and I make brief eye contact. It's too brief to arise suspicion from blondie, yet long enough for me to sense his indifference toward me.

His indifference.

Is it possible that the size of the male ego is so grand that he is not experiencing even the slightest amount of shame that he is not only on a date with someone else, but also that the last time he saw me, he couldn't get it up? Surely the male ego is not that grand.

I motion to Lynnette to go to the bathroom for an emergency meeting. It is decided that I should use the direct approach. By direct, I mean send him a text message right then and there as I sit on the faux-wood linoleum bathroom floor and watch Lynnette tease her wavy hair.

Me: Are you on a date?
Number Fifteen: Who is this?

And that is the story of how a man with erectile dysfunction decided he was too good to date the likes of me. I guess the male ego *is* that grand.

Date Sixteen: Single Dads with Divorce Guilt

I am done meeting men online. I will do it right. I will meet them in person. Meeting a man in person is a better bet. You can pick up on vibes from someone in person versus the unknown of what lies on the other end of a dating app.

So where does a thirtysomething, widowed, unemployed mother go to meet a decent man? Bars? No, they are all alcoholic limp dicks. Church? No, they are all arrogant, self-righteous porn addicts. The grocery store? No, they are all unhappily married. The gym? No, they all like to have sex in front of mirrors so they can watch their muscles flex the entire time while basically ignoring you and using your vagina as a masturbatory tool (true story).

I will meet men at my kids' school. Don't judge. It's not like I am winning any Mother of the Year awards lately anyway. I have been sucking at my motherly duties due to the one-year anniversary of my husband's death, which has retriggered my guilt and caused me to place an unfair distance between my children and myself, just to keep my grief from swallowing me whole.

My son wants me to volunteer at his field day, and I quickly agree, surprising us both as it is a well-known family fact that Mommy has major social anxiety at school functions. The thing that tipped me off was when he used the phrase, "All the dads will be there mostly helping, but moms can come too." Dads? Possibly single dads with divorce guilt who are compensating by being overly involved in their kids' lives? *Cha-ching!* I will volunteer the shit out of that field day.

And so I do.

Yes, my outfit is slightly inappropriate, but I justify it by complaining about the heat to the other appropriately dressed volunteers who have shirts with sleeves and everything. I make eye contact with Number Sixteen after his second lap around the track as he helps the kids with warm-up laps.

No wedding ring? Check.

Broad shoulders? Check.

Blond-hair, blue-eye combo? Check.

Looking at my legs? Double check.

Each time people round the fourth turn of the track, I am supposed to use my red Sharpie to put a dot on their hand, and then the teachers can tally up the number of laps they've accomplished. When Number Sixteen comes over to me, I put a heart on his hand. On the next lap, I write the number seven. And on the next lap, I write the number six, and so on, and so on, until my entire phone number is on his hand, and he is sweating profusely.

That night we go out for sushi. On the second date, we go to a movie, where we cuddle and kiss through the whole thing. On the third date, he has me over to his friend's house for a barbeque, and he cooks chicken especially for me.

When he walks me to my car, he gives me one of those "hair kisses"— you know, when a guy moves his hands up your back and into your hair? Yes, after the hair kiss, I decide that on the fourth date, I will have sex with him. I am doing this right! I am good at dating!

"Can I see you again tomorrow?" he asks.

"Yes," I say, smiling. When I get home, he calls me to make plans for our next date, and we end up talking until one o'clock in the morning. The next day, an hour before our date, I text him to see if I should bring a jacket or not, and I don't hear back from him. Ever.

A month later, I see Number Sixteen and his wife (whom he told me he was divorced from) holding hands and watching their son play soccer with my son on the field where we first met.

Date Seventeen: I Am a Slut

I am *still* done meeting men online. I will do it *right*. I will meet them in person.

I met Number Seventeen at a Starbucks. We both order unsweetened green tea and are amused that someone else on the planet prefers tea to coffee. On our third date, we kiss. Our first kiss feels like we have kissed a thousand times before. He feels so much like home to me that after a month of seeing him every day, and at his request, I let him come over and make dinner for my two kids and Lynnette's three kids. He's the first and only man I ever let that close to my little family of seven. Afterward, he plays football with all five of the kids in the street while Lynnette and I sip cocktails on lawn chairs. He even makes friends with my daughter's pet rabbit.

He repeats this routine every day for another month. He goes to work from eight to four during the day, stops by the grocery store, comes over, and cooks us all food. He then plays with the kids and, after everyone has gone to sleep, makes out with me on the couch downstairs. Then he goes home to his bed, and I go to mine.

After my first dinner with him and his parents, I decide the wait is over. It feels like we have had sex a thousand times before. He feels so much like home to me. He doesn't come over the next day to cook and play but asks if he can take me to celebrate my birthday with his parents on Saturday night.

He's different the entire night. I can feel it in the top part of my stomach, the exact center of my body. I confront him on the long, dark drive home. He denies any change. I look out the window, and tears fall from my eyes without warning. Suddenly, they are just there, and they are hot. This will all be over soon. The closest thing I have had to a boyfriend, to someone claiming me as his own, will be gone. He will pull away now and be cruel to me until I leave him so that I will shoulder the blame for our breakup. He will be like my husband in the months before I discovered his last affair—cold, indifferent, and accusatory.

So I end it with him. His parents get mad at me, and he won't defend me as they attack me on social media. A week later, he finally admits his lack of interest in me.

"I can't explain it," he tells me over *text message*. "After we had sex, it just didn't feel right anymore. I just lost my feelings for you, but I didn't know how to tell you." Then he offers me the consolation prize: "I still want us to be friends, though. I'd still like to come over and make dinner and play with the kids."

I don't ever see him again.

I hope to discover that he has a girlfriend when I stalk his social media; then this will all make sense. I did it the right way. I met a nice Christian man at Starbucks. We dated, got to know each other's family, and then became intimate. Doesn't that guarantee me a boyfriend for at least six months?

Every day after our breakup-or rather, fake-up since we were never official, he comes up with a new excuse as to why he can't come over to make dinner and play with the kids, while I cry to him and ask what I did wrong. Then one day he doesn't even text to give me an excuse.

Six months later, I get a Facebook message from Number Seventeen, who's obviously drunk. He says he hasn't gotten laid since we had sex and asks if I would please come over and fuck him because I am a slut.

No, you did not miss a part of the story. There is nothing imperative I have left out to make his cruelty toward me make sense. He dated me until I grew attached, slept with me after waiting for months, stopped liking me for no real reason, let his parents attack me, and then he himself attacked me.

He attacked *me*.

You can sleep with a man on a first date or do it the "right" way and sleep with him on the nine hundredth date, and he will still give himself permission to call you a slut, leave you, ignore you, choose another woman over you, and blame you. You can devote your life to a man, bear his children, cook his meals, and cultivate a loyalty to him so fierce that you abstain from masturbation for the entirety of your marriage. Still, he will give himself permission to call you a slut, leave you, ignore you, and then blame you for his infidelities and suicide.

There are two ways to react to this epiphany about men.

One way is to accept that using your own love and loyalty as manipulative tactics to gain the love and loyalty of a man is futile and will backfire. You can tell yourself that his actions toward you say more about who he is as a person than they say about your worth. You can accept that not all men are like this; there are men who will take the time to really see you, then love you, and then favor the way you smell after three days with no shower, over a clean woman wearing expensive perfume. You can accept that you have, in fact, gone on dates with men that had the potential to be this, but you rejected them because you are not ready to be loved because you simply aren't. Because enough time has not yet passed and healing has not even started because you don't yet believe that healing exists for someone like you. You can accept that men are not the only enemy, but women are too. You can accept that people lie, cheat, judge, harm, and, at their core, care only for themselves. You can accept that you are one of these people too. You can accept that our inability as the human race to overcome our selfishness is what binds together all humans that have ever or will ever exist.

Or you can refuse this acceptance and get angry.

Anger: ang-ger (noun)

Doing a lot of stupid shit.

Michelle, 33

...han a mile away   Active just...   Edit Info

5'4 125lbs....

Hate exercise, love food, so I'll be morbidly obese soon.

Outgoing introvert

Widowed once, divorced once, single Mom which means I am not relationshit material in the eyes of all men

Completely bitter

Please send me dick pics, gay websites pay me good money for them

My nude pics cost $2.5 million and aren't worth it due to my stretch marks and saggy mom boobs

Stop asking to do things to my butt that you won't let me do to yours

Date Eighteen: The Most Satisfying Part

I'm back to online dating because men are assholes no matter where you meet them.

Number Eighteen is twenty minutes late for lunch. Again. It's hot in my car, but I wait in the parking lot. I will not be the girl sitting in the restaurant alone. Again. He arrives after the fifth song on my Taylor Swift playlist with the same old apologies and a new pair of Ray-Bans.

"Let's go! I'm starving," I say.

"First, I have to show you something," Number Eighteen says mischievously. He uses his overwhelmingly large frame to guide my body to his truck despite my protests. He sits down on the leather seat and closes the door. The windows are overly tinted but provide little relief from the heat.

"What?" I say, hoping for some sort of gift. He raises one eyebrow and gives me a look like he knows I'm not wearing panties under my dress. He pats his lap and unzips his jeans. I hate him for his presumption, and I hate myself for my inability to say no.

I order the three most expensive tempura rolls on the menu, even though I know I can only consume one. Lynnette will love the other two. The roll that I do eat is the most satisfying part of that date. The shaft of his penis has hair on it.

Anger: ang-ger (noun) Doing a lot of stupid shit.

Date Nineteen: Choke Me

"Hit me," Number Nineteen says aggressively through gritted teeth. And so I do—on his shirtless back, which I have full access to because I am straddling him. "Harder," he says, coaching me, "with a closed fist," and so I do. I hit him and hit him and hit him again, increasing the intensity with each pound of my fist. It is freedom that I cannot injure him no matter how hard I try because he is so very large, and I am so very small, and I do try. With each blow, he moans in pleasure.

Men are sick.

"Pull my hair," he instructs. And so I do until I can feel every other hair follicle uprooting.

"Choke me," he begs. And so I do until I feel his pulse on the surface of his neck, as if it lives outside of his body.

"Bite me," he says. And so I do until I am sure my teeth will break the skin.

He can't restrain himself once my teeth pass the point of no return and leave a mark that will be part of his body for no less than a week.

When we finish at the same time, we finally open our eyes and look around. The tide has come in and is only a few feet from us. The fall moon is now directly overhead. Hours and hours have passed.

Today would've been my ten-year wedding anniversary. I want to raise my husband from the dead. I want to punch him until I knock the wind out of him, pull his hair until even his scalp is detached, choke him until he is decapitated, and bite him until all the blood from his body is gone.

I am sick.

Anger: ang-ger (noun) Doing a lot of stupid shit.

Date Twenty: Size Doesn't Matter

Number Twenty is looking at me lovingly, grazing my bare breasts with his fingertips. My skin is numb from the alcohol, so I can barely feel his touch. It's the middle of the day. The day is hot and long—the very opposite of his penis. What a waste of time he was. Why is he still here? Why is he looking at me? Are we supposed to have some sort of fucking conversation now? Maybe he can tell me his little hopes and dreams before he disappears to the island of men who forget they fucked me.

"I can't figure you out," he says. "Other girls I can read instantly, but with you, I just don't know."

I don't know why this statement angers me, but it does. Maybe it's because I woke up angry for the last one hundred days in a row, and I need someone to take it out on. Maybe it's preemptive, because it's only a matter of time before he does something to piss me off. Or maybe it's because men have freedom and women have emotions. Yes, that is it. He is free, and I am "cost"—today has cost me something. I know that doesn't make sense. But in my bedroom that day, a comparison between emotions and freedom or the lack thereof seems to sum up my life perfectly. So just go with it, and pretend this is a profound statement about feminism or something.

I catapult from my seated position among the pillows and unopened box of condoms. For the first time since he showed up in my room, I lock eyes with him. "What?" he says, startled by my abrupt alertness.

I don't answer him. Instead, I openly glare at him. I want to make him feel my hatred. Without blinking, I stare boldly into his empty blue eyes and yell loudly inside myself, "I fucking hate you! You are just like the rest of them!" No one hears this but me, and that makes me feel small.

He breaks eye contact as if he knows what I've just said to him inside my head, sits up, and excuses himself to go smoke. I lock the door behind him.

In my dreams that night, I am ripping out the hair from the head of one of my husband's affair partners and eating it while she screams for mercy. What a lunatic I am.

Anger: ang-ger (noun) Doing a lot of stupid shit.

Date Twenty-One: A Bar Fight

When a man is late for our date (which happens often when you "meet" men via free dating apps), I make it my goal to pick up another man before my date gets there. I had almost picked up the slightly overweight, balding businessman when Number Twenty-One finally graces me with his presence.

"You're late," I say.

"And you're more beautiful than I expected," he says charmingly. "Can I order you a drink?"

"I already bought the lady one," says the businessman.

Had it not been for his tardiness and the fact that he put his pinky up every time he sipped his fruity cocktail, I might have actually liked Number Twenty-One. But I know I won't, so I order the most expensive appetizer and the most expensive vodka for my martini. As the doomed date goes on, the businessman becomes drunk and obnoxious. He eavesdrops on us, inches his barstool closer to me, and joins our conversation, much to the obvious dismay of Number Twenty-One.

I really and truly hope these two get into a bar fight over me.

Sadly, they don't. Number Twenty-One maturely stands up after he finishes his drink and says, "Let's go somewhere else. Somewhere quieter." I do not want to go. I do not like Number Twenty-One. I want him to feel as shitty as I did sitting there at the bar by myself. I want him to pay for his sins and the sins of all the men in all the world who ever made a woman wait for anything. I want him to be emasculated, which I feel is the worst punishment for a man besides making him spend a bunch of money on you when you have no intention of ever seeing him again.

As I search my brain for a witty way to simultaneously dump and degrade him before I go home alone, the businessman notices we are about to leave. He stands up, hands me his card with his phone number circled on it as if Number Twenty-One does not exist, then tosses a fifty-dollar bill onto the bar between our drinks.

"My apologies for ruining your evening," he says to me, "but you deserve better."

Number Twenty-One has been emasculated, and I didn't even have to do it. Too bad the businessman was wearing a wedding ring.

Date Twenty-Two: I Want to Disrespect Him

I hate when I meet a man and know on sight that I won't like him, even if he is a nice, attractive man on his dating profile—for whatever reason, sometimes I am just not attracted to him. This is one of the major risks of online dating. Sometimes I just don't feel the biological, chemical thing that needs to happen for me to choose spending time with him over spending time in bed with my Jared Leto pillow, Netflix, and a sleeve or two of Oreo cookies. This lack of chemistry used to make me sad. Now, it just pisses me off. How dare he not produce the pheromones I need to make me attracted to him!

How dare he!

Number Twenty-Two walks in. Instantly, there's zero attraction—damn it! I'm immediately pissed. He's my fourth zero-chemistry date this week, and it's only Tuesday. It's not like I can just get up and leave the date or anything, though, so I have to sit and go through the rigmarole of the first-date question list. This is torture.

So, Michelle, what do you do for fun? Gee, Number Twenty-Two, I like to have sexual intercourse with bad-for-me men in the backseat of cars, drink vodka until I pass out, and spend money I don't have on clothes I won't wear more than once. What about you?

What exactly are you looking for in a man? Well, Number Twenty-Two, I'm glad you asked. I happen to be looking for an emotionally distant, arrogant prick who thinks he's the center of the damn universe. I want him to stick his penis in me and only me from now until the end of time, but never live with me, marry me, or desire to impregnate me. It's a bonus if he is an addict of some sort.

So, when was your last relationship? How long were you together? Why did you guys break up? My last relationship ended a year ago. We were together for ten years. He shot himself. So, yeah, that's pretty much how it ended.

Do you have children? I have two, and my domestic partner and BFF, Lynnette, has three. I basically have five children. They range in age from three to fourteen, and we all live in a nice little neighborhood where the children physically destroy our house, complain about chores every single day, and take all of our money. You will never meet them because they are too precious and wonderful and amazing to ever be introduced to someone who will probably have sex with me after two months and then never talk to me again. Oh, what's that you say, Number Twenty-Two? You can relate because you have three dogs? Of course you can! Parenting is the same as leaving an extra bowl of food out for your animals while you spend weekends away on business.

Needless to say, Number Twenty-Two won't be going on a second date with me. I hate having time away from my children wasted on a man who I'll never see again, while answering the same questions I already answered on my dating profile, which he obviously didn't read because he is shallow and only looked at my pictures.

When Number Twenty-Two gets up to go to the bathroom (also known as going to check his messages to see which of his other Tinder matches have responded to him), I turn to the stranger sitting to the left of me at the bar whose hand has been on my thigh the entire time I was on my date with Number Twenty-Two.

Oops! Did I forget to mention that?

Yes, about two sentences in with Number Twenty-Two, I purposely began rubbing my bare thigh against the guy sitting next to me until he gave in and put his hand on me. Fuck you, Number Twenty-Two!

"Excuse me. I'm not an armrest, you know," I say to the stranger.

"That wasn't my intention," he replies.

"What was your intention?" I ask.

"You tell me—you're the one who practically forced me to touch you."

"Who? Me?" I say with a faux innocence that neither of us buys.

"Let's not waste any more time; your little boyfriend will be back any second. How's about you give me your number, so I can start touching more than just your thigh?"

And so I enter my number into his phone under the name "Beyoncé" because, well, *Beyoncé*. I do this even though I feel no chemistry with the

Anger: ang-ger (noun) Doing a lot of stupid shit.

stranger and know I will ignore his text messages. I do this because I hate Number Twenty-Two so much for me not liking him that I want to disrespect him. Even though he never sees me get the stranger's number, I know that I do, and this expresses my anger at Number Twenty-Two and at all the men I do not like—for now.

Anger: ang-ger (noun) Doing a lot of stupid shit.

Dates Twenty-Three and Twenty-Four: So Very Hard

Number Twenty-Three is about to start his shift at the firehouse. He stops by to give me the *Hunger Games* DVD he borrowed last month. It's taken a month for him to return it because we cannot be within four feet of each other without him accidentally on purpose penetrating me, and we vowed that was never allowed to happen again.

He texts me from the car:

Number Twenty-Three: I'm outside. Come get the movie.
Me: Just bring it in. The door's unlocked, and I don't want to walk all the way to the fence in my heels.
Number Twenty-Three: Fine. I just got out of the gym. Can I change my clothes in the house, or are the kids home?
Me: I have the house to myself.

I'm wearing my red peep-toe sling-back heels and black leather leggings with a corset top. He is wearing sweaty, sexy gym clothes that fall over the form of his back muscles; muscles I have spent countless hours admiring and nibbling. But we will not have sex. We will not!

Number Twenty-Three and I have always been good at make-believe, and today we are make-believing that we both don't know why he came over. As he walks into my bedroom, he mentions that he has to be at work soon. I counter this by telling him I have a date soon. It will be easy to keep things platonic, we agree.

But Number Twenty-Three has never been easy for me. In fact, he has always been, well, hard—so very, very hard. And long. And thick.

Our clothes float like the parachutes you are allowed to play with in elementary school once a month for PE. They look slow and magical as they fall to the floor. As he finishes, I can see him in the reflection of the full-length mirror. He releases my hair and brings his mouth to the back of my neck. I can't feel either of these sensations, though, because I am numb and shaking.

Always, Number Twenty-Three anesthetizes me.

I hate that he has this power over me. I hate that his girlfriend is blond. I hate that this will be the last time I ever see him. I hate that I have developed the ability to know when a man is done with me. And he is done with me, but I am done with him too, so I decide to treasure the hickey he has just left on my neck until it fades.

An hour later, I am on a date with Number Twenty-Four. We have kids the same age. It's nice to talk to another single parent. But he has his kids half the week, and he and his soon-to-be ex-wife are the best of friends and coparent like they just popped out of some sort of healthy *How to Coparent Like Champs* instructional manual, whereas I have my kids full time and have no one to coparent with because the would-be coparent is dead. So, yeah, I guess I pretty much have nothing in common with a single parent…except for the fact that it is not strange to either of us later when I have to push his daughter's squeaky toy off his couch because it keeps jabbing my ass while we are having sex.

Our clothes don't float. They remain on our bodies, forced into positions that expose the necessary parts, and only the necessary parts. After he finishes, he pushes his index finger into the obviously fresh hickey that Number Twenty-Three left on the back of my neck a few hours before.

He laughs.

He gives me another hickey right next to it. "You can stay the night if you want, but I gotta get up early and go to work. My shift at the firehouse starts at 8:00 a.m.," he says as he disappears into the bathroom.

I'm driving home listening to Pink's album *The Truth about Love* before Number Twenty-Four even finishes his shower. Pink and I both know the truth now; that love does not exist in the ways we were brought up to believe. Love is no more than an evolutionary adaptation our brains have made to drive us into mating. "Love" is just a way Mother Nature has chosen to perpetuate our species. Love as we knew it was not only gone, but it was never even there.

Anger: ang-ger (noun) Doing a lot of stupid shit.

I knew this was the way things would end with Number Twenty-Three and Number Twenty-Four. I knew before I woke up this morning that I would conquer them both. I knew exactly what I was doing. I had been sober through all of it just so I could feel the immense satisfaction of turning these men into objects. I want them to tell each other about having sex with me. I want them to know that I had sex with them both on the same night within hours of each other. I want them to know they are not special. I want them to know they are worthless.

I feel powerful. This must be what it feels like to be a man, I think as the song *Slut Like You* plays.

Anger: ang-ger (noun) Doing a lot of stupid shit.

Date Twenty-Five: The Virgin Suicides

Number Twenty-Five and I take an Uber to a karaoke bar to meet Lynnette and her new boyfriend. I like Number Twenty-Five. I really, really like him. I like him so much that I want to introduce him to Lynnette. I like him so much I am not going to have sex with him tonight, even though I am wearing the cursed black leather leggings. This is the black leather leggings' first appearance since the double-firefighter fuck, and I have vowed that the leggings will not overpower me this time! I will beat the leggings. I will be a lady, in spite of them.

I lean over and put my head on Number Twenty-Five's shoulder. He is stiff, and I am awkward lying on him. "What's wrong?" I ask.

"I'm just not really into PDA," he says apologetically.

"It's just us and an Uber driver," I say.

"Yeah, I know. I'm just really not an affectionate person. It makes me uncomfortable." Number Twenty-Five is an emotionally distant asshole. Great. Now I'm in love with him. There is nothing sexier to me than an intimacy-challenged, impossible-to-tie-down, unaffectionate, uncompromising man.

Number Twenty-Five holds true to his word as the night goes on. Even with all the shots he's taking, he won't so much as allow our knees to touch under the table, even though no one would be able to bear witness to this meager show of affection. He is warm and personable and funny, though, and eases right into the conversations with Lynnette and her boyfriend. I am proud to be his date. We sing off-key, we dance with the confidence of toddlers who have the rhythm of rednecks. We take shots—lots and lots of shots.

Still, he will not touch me. I cry to Lynnette about this on the blue octagon-shaped industrial tile of the bathroom floor of that grimy karaoke bar. She too cries—about men, about money, and about how we were once beautiful and innocent.

I don't know if it was his rendition of Madonna's "Material Girl," or his refusal to even make eye contact with me all night, or the whiskey that was now seeping out of my pores (I have, since this night, banished any and all whiskey, indefinitely), but by the time the bartender yells out, "Last call!" I am ready to have sex with Number Twenty-Five on top of the bar for God and all the drunken people to witness.

But I won't. Even in my whiskey haze, I refuse to give in to my sick desire to conquer a man who has so physically and publicly rejected me. I do have some pride, after all.

You know what doesn't have pride, though? Those fucking black leather leggings! As soon as the car door closes and the Uber driver gets our destination address, Number Twenty-Five plunges at me like a chronically single veteran bridesmaid plunges at the flowers during the bouquet toss at the expense of hopeful little girls and her own dignity. "I couldn't stop thinking about your ass in those leggings all night," he whispers in my ear and then pulls my leggings down to my knees with his teeth. He expresses verbally his delight over the fact that I'm not wearing underwear and that I've just been waxed, as if the Uber driver is not even there.

It is when the driver politely turns up the music to drown out our increasingly loud moans that I consider the fact that Number Twenty-Five might not be an emotionally distant, unaffectionate asshole after all. Maybe his lack of PDA is some form of strategic-restraint foreplay for him. His lack of attention to me at the bar was so very obvious. At one point during the night, when I declined a drink from another man and told him I was on a date, the man looked at me in shock and said, "Really? I thought that was your brother or something." And now, Number Twenty-Five and I are being very un-sibling-like and breaking all kinds of public fornication laws in the backseat of a stranger's vehicle.

Yes, Number Twenty-Five wasn't an asshole—he was a foreplay genius!

When we pull up to his town house, Number Twenty-Five's shirt is off, and my pants are around my ankles. He picks me up (Number Twenty-Five, not the Uber driver) and carries me like a baby over to the grass, lays me down, and gets on top of me as the Uber driver leaves. It

Anger: ang-ger (noun) Doing a lot of stupid shit.

is pitch black. Even the two nearest streetlamps are out. I look up at the stars. I hope I remember this in the morning.

And I do. I think about it for days after—the shade of black the sky was, the warmth of his mouth contrasting with the night air, the smell of the grass, and The Cranberries "Linger" playing on the Uber driver's radio as he drove off. Apparently Number Twenty-Five is not as nostalgic. I don't hear from him for a month after this.

During that time, I wear the tan fleece blanket my husband and I got for a wedding gift as my shawl, and slipper socks as my shoes, as I read and reread the part in Jeffrey Eugenides's *The Virgin Suicides* when Trip Fontaine leaves Lux Lisbon on the football field. I connect with her in a way that I didn't thirteen years ago, when I first discovered this novel.

I know why Lux killed herself now, and I know why my husband killed himself too. They were consumed by rage—rage about the things people do and the brain chemistry that they could not control, rage about being abandoned, rage about not being able to change the things about themselves that they needed to change in order to keep their beloveds with them. While depression had made them both suicidal, rage had given them the courage to end their lives. And ending your life is as courageous as it is cowardly.

I pretend to be friendly when I get a text from Number Twenty-Five on the thirty-second morning after our sex-in-the-Uber date. I pretend to be the fun girl, the one who prefers casual sex and feels smothered by men who talk to her after dates. Fun Girl forgives and forgets, and then, Fun Girl goes back for more. I set up another date with him. Look at me, Number Twenty-Five! I am fun! I won't even require you to take me to dinner. I will deliver myself to your bed in red lingerie and waive the delivery fee.

Just.

For.

You!

When he falls asleep that night, I steal $127 out of his wallet before I sneak out, and I block his number from my phone. Good thing he never even bothered to ask me my last name and therefore can never find me to demand his money. Good thing he recently lost his job, and that $127 was probably his grocery money for the month.

I hope he starves to death.

I buy makeup with *my* money—the money that *I* earned. Applying my new cosmetics makes me wish I were brave enough to express my anger without passivity, but I'm not. The bravest thing I've done since my husband died is shower every other day, and some weeks, I don't even manage that.

Date Twenty-Six: He Climaxes

"**P**ut your finger in my ass," Number Twenty-Six says, to my surprise.

I knew there was a self-serving reason for him wanting to be on top. They never want to be face-to-face unless it serves them somehow. It's moments like these that really make you ponder the big questions in life. Questions such as, how is it that ass play has recently been moved from a taboo subject to the ever-growing list of accepted sexual practices (thanks, Internet porn!)? And, more importantly, will ass play ruin my fresh hot-pink manicure?

"Come on," he says. "Do it for me. Do it before your cab gets here. It'll be so fucking hot."

I search my mind for an acceptable excuse to not do this. Why is it that simply not wanting to ruin my manicure isn't an acceptable excuse? Why must I always be the yes-girl?

"I don't want to rush this. My cab will be here any minute. Maybe next time?" I ask, even though I know there will not be a next time. There is never a next time.

"I'll drive you home; just ignore the cab when it gets here." He will drive me home. Number Twenty-Six, whom I have made it to date number three with, will drive me home! This means more time alone with him to discuss our mutual love for burnt hot dogs and indie films! This means he really likes me! This means we might possibly have a fourth date! This means more time before my eventual banishment to the island of women he no longer wants.

And so I do it. I ruin my manicure.

He climaxes. Then there's the sound of a car horn. "Your cab is here—hurry," he says as he pulls out and sprints to the window to signal the cab driver with the condom still on his now-flaccid penis.

"I thought you were driving me home." And as soon as I hear my own words, I realize how naïve I was.

"Well…I don't really need to now, since we're done, and the cab is here," he says as he motions to the cab driver to wait.

"Can I at least wash my hands?" I say in an irritated tone. He matches my irritation with an eye roll.

"What? You're, like, mad or something?"

"Not at all," I lie. And I'm not. As a matter of fact, I feel happy after I go home that night and give his phone number and physical address to no less than thirty gay-porn sites.

Anger: ang-ger (noun) Doing a lot of stupid shit.

Date Twenty-Seven: I Smile

Number Twenty-Seven was embarrassed about his calloused weight-lifting hands. I don't know why. His fingers were long, and his touch was soft. He was gentle with me, tender and shy. He was nothing like his online persona had suggested. Why was he so insecure? Does he not realize the power a professional athlete has?

When we embrace under the stars on the perfectly manicured lawn of his suburban home for minutes before I leave, I spend those minutes thinking of how he will reject me within the next few days or weeks. None of them last more than a few sex sessions, which is a shame because after session four, most of my inhibitions cease to exist. But men are fickle and thrive on the chase of something new.

Right then and there, in his arms, I get angry with Number Twenty-Seven for his inevitable dismissal of me. He has no idea what he'll be missing, how far I would go to please him. I hate him. I hate them all.

As he rubs my back and breathes in my hair, I comfort myself with thoughts of how I will be a story he tells his upper-middle-class golf buddies at the country club one day. While his thin, blond, and educated wife in a floral skirt lounges in the club's restaurant with her sorority sisters, the retired athlete will entertain the other bored married men with tales of the inelegant, dirty brunette who gave him the best head of his life. His wife won't even get on top. I smile.

Anger: ang-ger (noun) Doing a lot of stupid shit.

Dates Twenty-Eight and Twenty-Nine: He Owns Me

Sex in a bathroom stall can be tricky. While not as slippery as shower sex, it still involves various standing positions, minimal space, and, in this instance, high heels. Number Twenty-Eight asked me to be his date to a wedding—on Valentine's Day.

Widows do not belong at weddings. Ever. Nor do they belong beyond the confines of a bar on Valentine's Day because widowhood does not go away. Widowhood does not care that it is Valentine's Day. I don't get a sanity break from being a widow. I am a widow on my birthday, on his birthday, on Flag Day, on Presidents' Day, on vacation, at baby showers, at fucking bridal showers, and at my kids' graduations.

I am a widow at 9:34 p.m. on a Monday, and I am a widow at 2:56 a.m. on a Saturday. I am a widow when I am sick and fatigued and dancing and showering. I am a widow the day I have to teach my son how to drive and my daughter how to flat iron her hair.

I will be my husband's widow even if I get a new husband. I will be his widow even on my own deathbed or in the car or at the grocery store or wherever death meets me. I will always belong to him and to this title that he has given me.

It is the same with infidelity. I will always be "the wife," the one who was stupid and blind and talked about behind her back. I will always be the one who was rejected, laughed at, loathed, lied to, and cheated out of the life that I signed up for. I will always be the one who was ignored at that party on Valentine's Day four years ago when I asked my husband where he and that one girl had disappeared to.

My husband's infidelities widowed me long before his suicide ever did.

And now that he is dead, I am still "the wife," and his death has now become the ultimate way for him to ignore me. I cannot fight with him. I cannot release my anger upon him. I cannot smell his neck and cry on his torso. I cannot strangle him to death. He is dead—forever. Even in my dreams, when I scream at him and throw Bibles and wine bottles at him, he ignores me.

He.

Ignores.

Me.

And Number Twenty-Eight ignores me too.

About five minutes into this blessed event, I realize that Number Twenty-Eight only invited me to have someone to stand next to him during pictures. Other than the few seconds it takes for the digital camera to capture all the falsities of a wedding, I am ignored. Cast aside. He wants me to stand next to him and look pretty. He wants me to keep my mouth shut except for when I am expected to laugh at his bad jokes and the bad jokes of his second cousin's third wife. He wants to introduce me to his relatives as a "friend," even though we've been fucking for more than a year.

I am his trophy, a monument that spends most of its time locked in a dark room, forgotten and collecting dust, only to be polished and shown off to family and friends on occasion to prove that he owns me. And he *does* own me, like my husband owns me.

But in that bathroom stall, I own him. I matter. I am the center of attention and not just the girl standing to his right. I am not his fucking friend. I am his girlfriend. Except I am not—I am never the girlfriend. I am "the wife"—the stupid wife.

We emerge from the bathroom and part ways. He goes to his group of friends (which happens to include one of my former lovers and his now-pregnant fiancée, because Valentine's Day isn't enough of a fuckery), and I go to the bar. I am shaking with suppressed rage—shaking. With the help of a slightly dirty martini with blue-cheese stuffed olives, I text Number Twenty-Nine.

By 9:00 p.m., Number Twenty-Nine and I are at a movie, and by 11:30 p.m., Number Twenty-Nine and I are passing his camera back and forth, taking pictures of each other in various sex positions. Number Twenty-Eight can ignore me all he wants. Vodka and I don't care—there are tons

Anger: ang-ger (noun) Doing a lot of stupid shit.

of other men who want me! In fact, they want me so much that they take pictures of me naked. Yes, Number Twenty-Nine is doing the opposite of ignoring me! He is memorializing me in photographs and no doubt showing these pictures off to all of his friends! He is excited to see me naked! He is going to remember this night forever! He is...passing out and snoring so loudly that I don't get to sleep.

Neither one of them gives me chocolates or flowers, but the combined forces of their semen give me a yeast infection. Happy Valentine's Day to me, and yet, I do not regret this, I decide on my cool, clean bathroom floor where vodka and I are napping later the next day.

I regret a lot of other things. I have regrets. I have them like I have freckles on my arms. They are part of me. I am completely confused by people who say they are without regrets because they are better people for their bad choices and circumstances. How do they know they wouldn't have turned out just as happy or good or whatever had they done or not done the thing they say they don't regret?

Yes, I have regrets. I regret getting married. I regret staying married. I regret finding those emails of my husband and all his women because that was the day I really became a widow. I regret asking him to tell me everything he'd been hiding because I can't unknow what I know now. I regret leaving him because if I hadn't he'd be alive. I regret not yelling at him when he was alive because now I have no one to yell at. I regret not telling the other women's husbands what they'd done with my husband because they are all still married, and I am not.

I regret how passive I was all those years before and after the affair discoveries. I regret not putting my husband's shit on our lawn when he cheated because then I had to sort through it and sell it when he died. I regret that we didn't even have a lawn because my husband spent all our money on his car hobby.

I regret my fears, all of them, because they held me back. And I regret every single tear I have shed over my husband because he is not worthy of them. I'm glad he's dead. And now, I regret saying that I'm glad he's dead because I'm not. But sometimes I am because I hate him so much.

No, I do not regret Numbers Twenty-Eight or Twenty-Nine. In fact, Number Twenty-Nine was so sweet he made me breakfast before I left. And by "breakfast" I mean a Pop-Tart. Even though he talked openly with me about his unrequited love for his ex-girlfriend and asked me for advice on how to win her back, he is not an insensitive asshole. Number Twenty-Nine is simply treating me the way I have taught him to treat me. They all are. And I am treating me how my husband taught me I should be treated with his "wife and widow" branding. This gives a dead man power over me. And this is depressing.

Depression: dih-presh-uh n (noun) Having enough energy for sex, but not enough for showers (unless you combine the two).

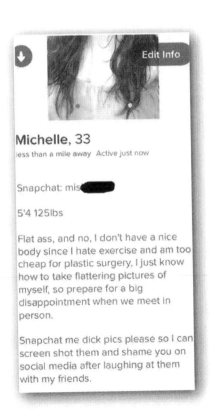

Michelle, 33
less than a mile away   Active just now

Snapchat: mis▮▮▮▮▮▮

5'4 125lbs

Flat ass, and no, I don't have a nice body since I hate exercise and am too cheap for plastic surgery, I just know how to take flattering pictures of myself, so prepare for a big disappointment when we meet in person.

Snapchat me dick pics please so I can screen shot them and shame you on social media after laughing at them with my friends.

Date Thirty: The Car Seat

Number Thirty and I have been friends for six months. We met because Lynnette and Number Thirty's best friend briefly dated after matching on Tinder, and the two of us were forced to accompany them on a double date once to ease the tension. Lynnette and Number Thirty's friend only lasted a few dates before he revealed to her that he was in fact twenty-two years old and not twenty-eight. Despite this, Number Thirty and I still hang out every so often and exchange pleasantries on social media. Nothing sexual ever happens, though. Our friendship is so platonic, in fact, that today we are discussing our sexual conquests while I am changing my clothes in front of him, and he's nursing a hangover with mimosas while stretched out on my bed.

We go out day drinking, just the two of us. It is hot, but in a refreshing way because we are exploring dive bars on the coast. Usually we are in a group, preventing us from any sort of verbal intimacy, but today we wander the streets of downtown together, lingering around pool tables and inactive neon signs. Our conversations get more personal after each set of double doors of the bars open, exposing our eyes to the unfiltered afternoon sunlight.

For the first time since we've known each other, the subject of my husband comes up. Number Thirty listens intently. I share with him my post-suicide crisis of faith, my loss of hope, and my uncertainty about my purpose in the world.

He reciprocates. He too has lost his faith in God and his hope in love, but he knows what his purpose in life is—his daughter. I had no idea he even had a daughter. This gives me a tenderness for him that's further increased as he goes on and on about his longing to be a good dad, his need to protect her, and his frustrations about the ongoing custody battle with her mother, his high-school sweetheart who cheated on him while he was stationed in Afghanistan.

Number Thirty gets it. He gets what it's like to be broken. He is like me.

"Do you ever regret having your kids so young?" he asks. "You know, because you, like, missed out on your twenties?"

"No," I say. "I loved being a young mother. I feel like I still had adventures in my twenties; they were just different ones than the adventure of the average twentysomething."

"Well put," he agrees. "I feel the same way about my daughter." We discuss at length the loneliness of single parenting and the fears we have for our daughters. We discuss how daughters need fathers, and sons need mothers. We discuss at what age daughters should start shaving their legs.

We go back to his house to nap off the buzz. I can never sleep next to a man, but with Number Thirty, that is not the case. We fall asleep on opposite sides of his king-size bed and wake up hours later, sober-ish and in each other's arms. We are equally surprised.

This begins a three-hour-long cuddle session, something I have not had in years, literally. None of the men I've been with have touched me longer than it has taken for them to get off. And the last three years of my marriage were shit. While my husband and I still maintained an active sex life, the tenderness was noticeably absent after the discovery of his affairs. I can only recall a lengthy cuddle session with him one rainy day in November back in 2010. That was five years ago.

Number Thirty and I use our fingertips to explore the nooks and crannies of each other's shirtless bodies, mostly staying clear of our genital regions. We kiss, we giggle, we tease, and we kiss some more. Could it be that all along Number Thirty and I were meant to be more than friends? How could I have missed this? Why is he suddenly so attractive to me? We don't have sex, but he wants to. If I weren't on my period, I would have.

Lynnette is suspicious right away when I tell her about my day with Number Thirty and the revelation about his daughter. "Michelle, he has a motorcycle, a part-time job, and three roommates. There is no way he has his child for half the week. Where the hell would he put the car seat?"

I am always the victim of my own naïveté and optimism.

Upon further research, we discover my friend Number Thirty made up having a child to try and sleep with me. He saw a vulnerable spot when I shared with him my sad little suicide-widow story, and then he attempted to create a bond through our mutual single-parent struggles.

And a bond *was* created by him, but he was not part of this bond. Even though I know everything was a lie now, I am still tethered to him. Boys can choose to bond and break bonds. Women cannot.

Boys are geniuses. Boys don't give a fuck about your sad story. They have the advantage, and they take advantage. They are the stronger sex. My learned sweetness combined with my inherited female need to connect is life-threatening. Connection is what caused me to be hospitalized after my husband's affair revelations. It is what would give me the instinct to step in front of a moving train for my children. It is why I vomit when I am rejected by a boy. It is what will cause me to be sad every single time I see my friend Number Thirty after this. It is what will cause me to text Number Thirty after bad dates to come over and cuddle me. And when he does, this bond I formed will be the reason that I pretend that all the things he told me were true.

Date Thirty-One: Blonde

He was a sweet country boy. Those accents always fool me.

> Number Thirty-One: I miss you! When are you coming back
> to visit?
> Me: Next summer?
> Number Thirty-One: Not soon enough. I need sex before that.
> Me: Go on Tinder and get sex. I can't afford another vacation
> until next year.
> Number Thirty-One: But I don't want a Tinder whore. I want you!
> Me: LOL "Tinder whore." Okay, maybe I'll come out sooner.

The next morning, Number Thirty-One has updated his Facebook status to "engaged," and his fiancée is the same shade of blond as one of the women my husband fell in love with. I don't shower for a week.

When I was seven, or maybe eight, years old, I experienced my first bout of depression. I don't remember the depression part, just coming out of it. I woke up one morning and it was very cold, so I put on my blue fuzzy slippers. My mom had the wood-burning stove going, and she greeted me with a blanket, pulled a chair in front of the warm stove, and served me hot chocolate and churros. I felt relief, like the black cloud had lifted, and I smiled while I ate. I felt happy again. I didn't even realize I had been sad until the burden of it had been lifted and then after this day when I experienced depression for days and weeks, I could identify this melancholy because I remembered the opposite feeling I'd had with the churros. I tried to recreate this feeling throughout my childhood, asking my mom for churros, hot chocolate, and a blanket, and she'd oblige, but I never found relief using this method again.

Boys always worked, though, even when I was eight years old. They always took me out of my depression. They also usually caused it.

Date Thirty-Two: I Pretend He Died

When The Killers perform my favorite of their ballads, "Here With Me," I begin to cry. Almost all live music has this effect on me, but this song in particular because of what it had once meant to my husband and me. It is chilly now that the sun has gone down, and the baggy thrift-store flannel over my tube top isn't doing much to quench the chill that is spreading over my body. One of my tears falls onto my right combat boot.

I have been missing my husband lately, and I don't know why. How can I possibly miss someone who cheated on me, then when confronted about it told me he never loved me, and then killed himself when I finally mustered up the courage to leave him? How can I miss someone who hated me so deeply?

I guess I just miss the man I thought he was before he became the man who obliterated me. I guess I just miss being married—the simplicity of it, the familiarity, the illusion of control, the robotic sex. I have never been adventurous or spontaneous or edgy. And dating in your thirties in San Diego is nothing short of adventurous and spontaneous and edgy. It is a cutthroat minefield that usually ends with a picture on social media or a visit to your local Planned Parenthood.

I just want to be married again.

When Number Thirty-Two returns with our margaritas, he notices the tear streaks on my face. He kisses them, wraps his arms around me, and says, "You're the only one I would ever bring to something like this. You're the only one I want with me right now. You get it. You get the music. I'm going to take you to every concert with me this year. It's going to be fucking epic." I am warm now, even though the margarita is cold as it travels through my veins.

When I leave Number Thirty-Two's bed the next morning, I know I won't hear from him again. And I don't. Maybe I'm bad in bed, which would explain why I never hear from these men after we have sex. No, my ego decides, that can't be it. Instead, I pretend that he died in a horrific car accident on his way to pick out flowers for me, and this is a better feeling than his abandonment.

Date Thirty-Three: Shower Sex

I'm not a believer that good shower sex exists. First of all, my make-up always streaks down my face, making me look like a clown or a drowned rat, and second, it usually involves a bunch of awkward and slippery standing positions. Number Thirty-Three makes me a believer, though—twice.

The steam. The water pressure on newly discovered erogenous zones. The shower curtain being used as a restraint.

A week later he is in the top of my Instagram news feed, down on one knee, proposing to the woman he told me was his platonic roommate. He gave her a three-stone diamond ring with a platinum band, just like the one my husband gave to me so many, many years ago.

Date Thirty-Four: My Life

I used to take two-step lessons. It is shocking that they even offer such a thing because this dance is so ridiculously simple. Still, I never could quite get it right. The problem is that I have issues with control (shocking, yes, I know). I can't relax and let a man lead me backward around a dance floor; I need to be in charge. Number Thirty-Four has been informed of this fact via text message, but he still insists on taking me two-stepping. He is unbelievably patient with me. I step on his feet the drunker I get, and I think that at one point I even insult and blame him for me not being able to maneuver properly. Still, he dances with me.

That night in bed (okay, on the staircase), he is polite enough to use his jacket as a pillow underneath my ass so I don't get rug burn. When he finishes, he says, "I'm really starting to like you. Like, really a lot. Come to a wedding with me next weekend. I'd love to introduce you to my family."

The things men say in the dark are the cruelest of all.

Number Thirty-Four is not starting to like me. He doesn't want me to meet his family. He simply wants someone to stand next to him and wear a pretty dress, probably to make some ex-girlfriend or bridesmaid jealous, and he wants me to fuck him later on, after the reception and open bar have come to an end.

I know the way men see me. I know my place in this world. I am not girlfriend material. I am not loveable. What he is saying to me is a lie.

The next morning, I wake up with a rash on my chest. It is in the exact shape of the exposed skin from my scoop-neck floral-print dress that I wore last night. The rash grows worse over the next five days.

I go to see the doctor, who prescribes a steroid cream and an oral antihistamine. "You are having an allergic reaction, but it should clear up within a few days."

I have had an allergic reaction to a man who is really starting to like me and to something as simple as two-stepping. What an appropriate metaphor for my life.

Date Thirty-Five: Salt

Salt water from the ocean gushes up the back of my white sundress when the tide comes in. We lose all track of time once Number Thirty-Five gets on top of me and starts kissing my neck as the sun fades into the other side of the world. Then we go to his truck, where our clothes became wet with the merging of our sweat and the salt water that saturates our clothing. The smell of the salt makes me high.

He pauses in the back of his truck during and looks at me. I break the silence. "What is your name again?" I ask him. He smiles in a way that I won't ever forget and then tells me his name, first and last.

"What's your name again?" he asks me.

"Michelle Miller," I say.

"That's a beautiful name," he whispers as sweat from his forehead drips onto mine.

And I'm glad I didn't make him wait. I'm glad I did it the wrong way. Either way, he would've never contacted me the next day. None of them do.

Date Thirty-Six: How Did He Die?

"So your Tinder profile says you work in marketing?" I say.

"Yeah, I've worked for my company for the last six years. My long-term goal is to open my own firm. What do you do for a living?" Number Thirty-Six asks.

"I don't work."

"Oh, that's cool. Why not?"

"I don't need to."

"Trust fund?"

"No."

"Alimony?"

"No. And no, I'm not a stripper, drug dealer, prostitute, or lottery winner, either."

"Okay, ha-ha. You get those questions a lot?"

"Yeah. I think men are just worried that I'm looking for a sugar dad-dy or something, so I get why they want to know, but, seriously, I'm financially independent and just looking for companionship, not money."

"So are you going to tell me where you get your money from?"

"You really wanna know?"

"Yes." He leans forward.

"My husband died last year. I'm living off the death benefits for the next few years, so I can be home more for my kids."

"I'm sorry to hear that. Was he a soldier?"

"No."

"Was he sick?"

"No."

"How did he die?"

"Suicide."

He leans back. "Oh, I'm sorry."

"It's fine. I'm okay talking about it. I just don't like to bring it up because it makes other people feel awkward, and it's kind of a conversation stopper. Like now. So, Number Thirty-Six, I'm going to go to the bathroom, and when I get back, you'll have come up with a new and lighter conversation for us to have, okay?"

"Ha-ha, okay, sure thing."

When I come back to the bar, Number Thirty-Six is gone. He still paid for my drink though. I went home with the bartender that night. He didn't ask me any questions.

Date Thirty-Seven: Alive in the Candlelight

What Number Thirty-Seven understands about sex is that it is not just the act. It is not just the "during." It is "before," and it is "after." It is all the things leading up to it, and it is all the things descending from it. Most men his age don't get that. Maybe it's because he is foreign. Maybe I do like Tinder after all.

Number Thirty-Seven's Australian accent, paired with his guitar-plucking fingers and attention to detail, creates the best faux intimacy I've had since my husband. The tattoo of a woman on his left bicep seems to be alive in the candlelight, and I'm not even drinking. Her eyes look frightened and young—vulnerable. Or maybe I just see art through my own experiences.

I ask him to leave the hotel suite when we are done. I never sleep well next to a man I don't know, and I don't know any of them. The next morning, I notice Number Thirty-Seven left cash for me on the night-stand. I should feel degraded—used. I don't. I feel powerful, attractive, and amused.

The more men I collect, the more I miss my husband. The more men I collect, the more healed I am from his rejection of me, and I don't even believe in healing.

Acceptance: ak-sep-tuh ns (noun) Giving up, but in a good way.

Michelle, 33
High School

📍 Location

ⓘ Info

5'4 125lbs, snapchat: mis (no, as a matter of fact, I don't want to see your penis)

I have 2 kids (go ahead and swipe left now), I've been widowed for 2 years (seriously, swift left!) & recently came to terms with the fact that I suck at dating. Good luck if you take me out!

Date Thirty-Eight: They Too Are All Naked

The beach:

Peace.

Clarity.

Salt.

The warmth of the sun melts my goose bumps. The creamy, moist sand gliding off the top of my toes is weightless with each step I take toward the indigo-and-jade-studded ocean. My hair is like cool, fresh silk that swishes back and forth on my bare, sun-kissed back.

I am naked.

There is no one around for miles, but I do not feel alone.

It is silent, the kind of silence in which you can't even hear your own thoughts—the kind of silence in which you have to put your hand on your chest to feel it rising and falling, so you know there is life going in and out of your body.

And then the bombs start dropping. They're black spheres at first, landing like raindrops on the serenity of the beach and the ocean, making the exact sound of my husband's shotgun. Panic comes over me in an instant, and I want to run from the fear, but the beach has turned to tar—heavy, thick, black, clumpy tar that encases my feet and keeps me from escaping.

I try to close my eyes because I know what is coming next, but my body was created without eyelids. I never had them, even though I have the instinct to shield my eyes with the loose, ocular skin patches that other people have. My eyelids just aren't there, and they never were.

It is coming. It is coming next. I know which part is coming next, and I cannot stop it. The black spheres cease. Silence. Then, everyone I love, everyone I have ever known since birth, emerges from the black tar of the beach. As far as I can see there are people somehow connected to me—through blood, through work, through a glass of wine we once shared, through playdates, and through grocery-store checkout lines. All of them, like meerkats sensing danger, slowly rise from the earth and look around before they fix their eyes on me—for help.

They too are all naked.

Then the firebombs start. They make the same sound as my husband's shotgun but magnified times infinity, mixed with the pitch of the last thing I heard from him before he took his life—screams. The spheres don't land on the meerkat people; they land next to them in the tar, and sizzle. I watch. The heat from the firebombs spreads up their bodies, its tentacles melting the flesh off their bones in increasingly slower motion.

The slower the flames crawl, the more pain my loved ones are in, and their pain leaps from inside their bodies to mine as if they are throwing it at me. Or maybe I take it from them. Yes, I take it. I steal their pain from them. The meerkat people know that I will consume their afflictions because I caused them. I am to blame for all of it—the tar, the spheres, and the pain. They all belong to me.

Still, even with their pain inside my body, they suffer. Nothing takes away their pain, even after I absorb it through my pores. I can't do anything right. I can't hear all the screams of every individual on the beach, but I know the words they are mouthing to me.

Accusatory words.

Sentences of discontent.

Paragraphs that will become part of the internal dialog I have with myself daily, which determines who I am.

No words are as clear as the ones forming on my children's lips, my children who are right in front of me—my children whom I cannot reach. "Mom! Save me!" they cry out to me in confusion and anger and brokenness. I want to explain to them about the tar that is submerging my feet and the invisible force that has now amputated my arms. I want to tell them that I am trying to save them, but I can't because my body has been mutilated and the pain has paralyzed my insides. The pain.

The. Pain.

The Pain.

THE PAIN.

As the flames continue to ascend my children's frail, charred naked bodies, all I can do is scream. No sound is coming out, but I scream anyway. My screams will not save them, even if they had sound, but I scream anyway. My screams will not communicate to them all the complex ways in which they are loved, but I scream anyway. I need them to know before the flames engulf them that they are loved—that they always have been, even before their conception.

I watch as their little faces, which I spent hours memorizing when I nursed them as babies, become mutated by the sheer force of their screams and then by the sheer force of the fire. What remains of their faces melts away, and their entire beings become one with the tar beach. I stopped long ago trying to close my phantom eyelids and can see, in excruciating detail, the molecules of their lives becoming indistinguishable with the tar on the beach. And there, inside myself, I choose to die.

The bombs and the noise cease.

I do not choose life anymore as I did on the cliffs with Number Four so very long ago. I am no longer in a state of denial. I can fully comprehend now how very bad everything is. And so I choose to die once my children have vanished into the beach—not because my children are gone, but because even before the flames engulfed them, I was not alive.

There is nothing but meerkat people for miles, but I feel alone. I want to shoot myself so my arms reappear. I want to do it with my husband's gun, so the gun appears. I aim it at my torso. I eagerly pull the trigger.

Pain.

It's the pain of everyone in the world who has ever existed, of the massive tar blanket of sand on my feet, of the shards of bullet that left my husband's gun ricocheting inside my body with no outlet. There will never be an outlet. I scream; only this time, I can hear my screams.

And then, I hear someone's voice, a man's voice. "Shhhhhhhhhhh," the voice says. "Hey! Wake up! Shhhhhhhhhhhh! Stop screaming!" It is Number Thirty-Eight, and I am in his bed after a long night of pizza and dry red wine. "What the fuck? You're gonna wake my roommates up!" he says quickly.

I am drenched in sweat—drenched. I have chewed the inside of my mouth and can taste my blood. My throat is dry. "I'm sorry," I say, out of breath, not quite sure if I am still in the dream or not. "I just have bad dreams sometimes." He falls back asleep on the other side of the bed without so much as a comforting word.

I'm too scared to be embarrassed; that will come later. I can feel the residual pain from the bullet in my nightmare darting around my body like dull needles poking me from the inside. I run naked to his bathroom and vomit. I spend the rest of the night on the urine stained bathroom floor. I'm too scared to leave his apartment in the middle of the night, so I stay there until dawn and sneak out at first light. I'm sure he is relieved to wake up to an empty bed.

It is the two-year anniversary of my husband's death, and I need help.

At the mere admission of this need, things began to change. Wait, no—I only wrote that because it sounded profound. The truth is, things did not magically change after I finally admitted to myself that I needed help. The truth is that I still went on a lot of shitty alcohol-fueled dates after this day, but my reactions to them began to change, and this was, so far, the closest I had come to healing.

I am deeply proud of this.

Date Thirty-Nine: Hired a Hooker

I've never been in a penthouse suite in Las Vegas until today. I feel like Vivian in *Pretty Woman* after she takes off her blond bob wig to reveal a crazy frizzy mass of red curls while floating around in the massive bathtub. I always liked that about Vivian, how after she serviced Edward, she wasn't intimidated by her luxurious surroundings.

Sex empowered her and depleted her simultaneously.

Today I pretend I am Vivian, except I'm not in the bathtub; I'm roaming around naked, looking for souvenir toiletries to steal, and the frizzy mass of curls on my head is dark brown, not red.

Number Thirty-Nine ran (literally) down the stairs to get the condoms I insisted on. What a good boy. When I hear the door handle turn, I hastily close the medicine cabinet I was going through (hemorrhoid cream!) and jump back into the king-size bed of the third bedroom on the right side of the hallway. I get into position (spread eagle) and listen for him.

Only I don't hear *him*. I hear *them*. I estimate there to be at least a dozen loud masculine voices coming in through the main entrance of the suite. I go from spread eagle to under the covers before I can blink, suddenly aware of how very naked I am. Where the fuck is my dress? What do I do? What would Vivian do?

Vivian would have strutted down the hallway naked, demanding her garment. I am not Vivian. I have not yet learned how to use my sexuality to my own benefit instead of for a man's benefit. I am still living under the fear of the empty space between my legs and my perception that men are determined to punish me for an anatomy I have no control over.

The loudest of the dozen voices notices my dress on a chair in the formal dining room and calls everyone's attention to it. They all begin calling out to Number Thirty-Nine, asking him if he has a girl up here, asking if they should leave, asking if the girl has some friends for them.

I stay silent.

They start going room to room, looking for the owner of the petite floral dress. With each turn of each doorknob I cringe. When the owner of the voice, a tall, sandy-blond, frat house–looking guy with abnormally broad shoulders gets to my room, he leans against the doorframe and stares at me with a grin.

"Hi. I'm a friend of Number Thirty-Nine," I say.

"Yes, I assumed," he says, making no attempt to mask the fact that he is looking at the shape of my body through the covers. He twirls my dress.

"Can I have my dress, please?" I plead.

"Oh, is this yours?" he teases. "You want this?" I nod. "Come and get it, darling."

"Just toss me my dress. Number Thirty-Nine will be here soon anyway, and we have a dinner reservation." My heart is racing at the realization of what a vulnerable position I've put myself in. I know he can sense my fear, and it's as if my fear feeds his desire to cause more of it. He stands there in the doorway, twirling my dress, taunting and laughing.

"Hey, homos!" he eventually yells down the hallway. "Number Thirty-Nine hired a hooker! Come see!" At the sight of a dozen (probably horny) men, my fear peaks. I am shaking under the covers as they begin peppering me with questions about my skills and rates. Number Thirty-Nine is not going to save me anytime soon. That idiot probably can't find any condoms; he probably has no clue what they look like because he's likely never had a girl make him use them.

Come to think of it, Number Thirty-Nine was the first man I stood my ground with when it came to condom usage. Thirty minutes ago, we were rolling around naked in the dining room when he tried to penetrate me. "No," I said. "Not without a condom." He pleaded and begged for nearly ten minutes, using every line I've ever heard about how he gets tested for STIs all the time, he's very healthy, he hasn't had sex in six months, he promises to pull out…blah, blah, blah. I had both of my hands over my vagina during his speech and refused him entrance until he had a condom on.

I was so done with STI tests and Googling vaginal discharge colors and their meanings and peeing on pregnancy tests and losing sleep over my fears about disease and pregnancy, in addition to my (soon-to-be-diagnosed) PTSD. I was done letting men take my peace of mind. I was barely sleeping more than two hours a night, and I would not have those precious two hours taken from me by fears that could be alleviated by Number Thirty-Nine wearing a (small) latex condom.

Recalling the image in my head of Number Thirty-Nine running out of the room to get condoms just to appease me gives me such a sense of confidence that suddenly I know just how to handle this group of horny, power-hungry men.

"Come on, sweetie. How much?" the short, muscular one repeats as I come out of my condom-insistence memory.

I sit up tall, purposely exposing my breasts. Just for extra impact, I roll my eyes. "You can't afford me," I say.

"Try me," he says, challenging me.

"Listen, sweetheart," I begin in a mocking tone, "I'm sure your little nine-to-five suit-and-tie job thingy can pay for a few extracurricular activities, but it's not going to cover the fee I'll have to charge you for me to fake an orgasm." All the men start laughing. "I'm not that good an actress," I add.

We all know I'm not really a Las Vegas prostitute. For one thing, my breasts are obviously natural, and for another, Number Thirty-Nine is too attractive to hire one. Their questions about my skills and rates were about them making fun of my precarious situation. Once I turned the tables on them and exerted confidence rather than fear, they had no choice but to back off.

There is a slight shift in the first guy's demeanor, which only he and I detect. I'm not afraid anymore. I can be naked in a room full of men and hold my own, and we both know it. "Now run along. I have actual business to attend to when Number Thirty-Nine gets back," I say. "And bring me a bottle of water. I'm parched."

The guy laughs as he tosses me my dress, as if to say, "Well played." He brings me two bottles of water and doesn't comment on the fact that I didn't even bother to put my dress back on or cover my breasts. The boys all leave me alone until Number Thirty-Nine gets back with a huge box of condoms—ribbed for *her* pleasure.

The whole time we are having sex, I ponder how much power I have and why I never thought to demand more from men. Thinking about this is a huge aphrodisiac. If I am worthy of condoms and bottled water and respect, maybe one day I will be worthy of love too.

Date Forty: Too Good

Just when I think I am over these stupid walking-on-the-beach-at-sunset dates, Number Forty changes my mind. He's not just walking with me on the beach to get a free date like so many men I've met online have before; he is genuinely in awe of nature and is discussing his passion for it in detail with me.

Finally, I'm out with a thoughtful, intelligent, sophisticated man. He is older than me and mature. I am on my best behavior as to not let on that I am a bitter, uneducated, unsophisticated, slightly crazy girl who he will eventually find he has nothing in common with.

He's too good for me.

"I'm really enjoying your company, Michelle. Would you mind staying later with me and watching the sunset?"

"I'd like that," I say in my best virginal, sweet, I-didn't-just-have-phone-sex-with-Number-Thirty-Seven-an-hour-before-this-date   voice. He guides me up the stairs to the lifeguard tower and, without me asking, puts his jacket over my shoulders and draws me into his body. The warmth of him is more soothing than the ocean.

"I have something for you," he says. And he reaches into his pocket and reveals a Snickers peanut butter candy bar. I think I actually start applauding with excitement. "I remember your Tinder profile says that the way to your heart is with chocolate." I thank him and happily eat my chocolate while gazing off into the hot-pink-and-blood-orange sky in front of me.

"I have something else for you," he says. And I can feel him rummaging through his pant pockets again, but I can't take my eyes off the way the sky seems to be alive, and we are the only two on earth who know this truth.

Then he is still. "What is it?" What other treat does Mr. Sophisticated have for me? Maybe it is a Kit Kat. A Kit Kat would perfectly complement my Snickers.

And so I turn around with all the anticipation of a child on Christmas morning who is about to be in possession of not one, but two candy bars. I turn to Mr. Sophisticated to find—

His penis.

His medium-size, fully erect (and curved to the left) penis. He begins to stroke it.

I am at the bottom of the lifeguard tower so quickly that I leave my half-eaten Snickers bar behind (a true testament to how very disgusted I am). "Wait!" he calls after me. "Come back! I'll put it away! It was only a joke!"

I run to my car and never return his texts and phone calls.

I'm too good for him.

Date Forty-One: A Truly Beautiful Woman

We are naked on an oversized white armchair, me on top (as usual), straddling him face-to-face. The bay windows are open, letting in the cool night breeze, fresh from the visible ocean. Our background music is the people on the sidewalk below us chattering over the melody of Taylor Swift's "Crazier," which is playing on his iPod. Number Forty-One forces me to pause, gently pressing my body down by my shoulders. He leans back, away from my chest, lights a cigarette, and looks me up and down. He's still hard, inside me. He gives me a look as if to say, "Don't worry; we're not done yet."

"You don't exercise at all, do you?" As he lights the Marlboro Red, he references our first-date conversation in which I performed a ten-minute dissertation on why I hate exercise.

"You know the answer to that," I say as I braid my hair.

"So you just naturally have this body?" He blows smoke rings to the right of me. I look down at myself. There are a few mild stretch marks below my belly button, a mild "mommy pouch," sweat dripping between my natural size-C breasts, and smooth olive skin over my thighs. For the first time since discovering my husband's affairs five years ago, I realize I am satisfied with the view of my naked body. What a strange feeling that is.

"Yeah, I guess." I lean back and grab the wine bottle from the coffee table behind me.

"No plastic surgery either?" He reaches for the bottle with his free hand.

"Nope," I say, pulling the wine farther away from him. He gives up on the wine bottle when I empty it into my mouth and lets his eyes wander over my torso. He visibly enjoys the nicotine rush while his right hand wanders up and down my bare back. I take the cigarette from his lips and put it to mine.

Inhale.

Exhale.

God, I miss smoking.

"You are a truly beautiful woman," Number Forty-One concludes after several seconds of observation. Maybe it is the timing, maybe it is the way he says it, or maybe it is just the truth, but I believe him. He's not the first to tell me something like this, but he is the first I choose to agree with. He takes the cigarette from my lips, puts it out in the empty wine bottle behind me, and encourages me to start moving up and down again.

There was never anything wrong with me or my body that caused my husband to cheat. It was his insecurities, his fears, and his hatred of himself that lead to his chronic unfaithfulness all those years. It's not my fault that my husband lacked the ability to appreciate the truly beautiful woman he was married to.

Date Forty-Two: Good in Bed

Number Forty-Two says, "Oh my God, *stop!*"

"What? Is everything okay?" I ask.

"Yes...it just feels too good...wait a minute." There's an awkward silence. "Okay, go...wait. Stop again! *Fuck!*"

"How about I just go slow?"

"Okay...wait!"

"What now? I was going slow!"

"High five!"

Our palms make contact in the air after a long pause during which I ask myself if he really just asked to high-five me during sex. Yes, Michelle. Yes, he did. I guess I no longer have to wonder if I'm good in bed or not.

Date Forty-Three: Channing Tatum

Number Forty-Three has the most beautiful face I've ever seen. I'm pretty sure I blush while stalking his social media. He is a male model—a legitimate runway model (insert *Zoolander* joke). His pictures and fifteen-second video clips have kept me company after many, many bad dates. If only I could print his pictures on a pillowcase and cuddle him every night, my loneliness would be cured.

I press the "like" button on most of the pictures he posts and make witty comments on his runway videos, even though I know someone as gorgeous as him will never even notice me among his thousands of Instagram followers. One night, after my third date in a row this week refused to pay for my cocktail, I press the "like" button on one of Number Forty-Three's Mark Wahlberg–inspired photo-shoot posts. A second later, I get a direct message from him and then a second later, a "follow" request.

Number Forty-Three wants to follow little ol' me? I accept his request and give him adequate time to scroll through my flawless, overly filtered, and completely unrealistic collection of social-media selfies before I look at his message.

After ten minutes and him liking eight of my selfies, I open his message with my heart racing like it did when I went to an *NSYNC concert for my sixteenth birthday. Yes, I was one of those girls; don't judge. You know you would've jumped at the opportunity to see the pelvic-thrusting dance moves of those boy-band members in the nineties too, even the one who eventually came out as gay (who, by the way, was my favorite, because my bad taste in men goes back long before the death of my husband).

Number Forty-Three: So, when are we hooking up?
Me: It's nice to meet you too, Number Forty-Three. Me? Oh, well, thank you so much for asking! I'm doing well, thanks. How about you?
Number Forty-Three: You don't strike me as the type for pleasantries, Michelle. Let's get to the point. There is a mutual attraction. Let's do something about it.

Me: Using my name—I see you've been well trained in the ways of seduction, my friend.

Number Forty-Three: Likewise, Michelle.

Me: Good Night, Number Forty-Three.

And then a week later:

Number Forty-Three: When are you coming over?

Me: Do you normally get women to come over to your house so easily?

Number Forty-Three: Women always cum easily with me.

Me: Is that a fact?

Number Forty-Three: I guess you'll just have to find out, won't you, Michelle?

Me: Fine. Meet me at Compass at nine tonight.

Number Forty-Three: Seriously?

Me: Yeah.

Number Forty-Three: Are you being serious right now, or am I going to show up and you won't be there?

Me: Why wouldn't I be there? Like you said, I'm not into pleasantries. I'm more of a cut-to-the-chase kind of girl. There's a mutual attraction, so let's meet.

Number Forty-Three: Okay, see you soon.

Me: I'll be the one in the black leather leggings and leopard-print heels.

Number Forty-Three: No top?

Me: Probably not. I haven't decided yet.

Number Forty-Three: See you soon.

Number Forty-Three has the most beautiful body I have ever seen. I'm pretty sure I blush when I remove his clothing. And I'm pretty sure I gasp when I see the size of his dick—three inches, tops. They must have used Photoshop on his bulge during those Marky Mark pictures. That's okay; it's not the size, but what he can do with it.

Turns out he can't do anything with it, or if he can, he refuses to show me. He refuses to get on top. I thought the first time he said no to my "get on top" request that he was joking, but after the second time, I know he is not a funny man—he is an asshole man. He lies on his back, hands behind his head.

"It's not going to suck itself," he says as he looks down at his Vienna-sausage dick and smiles.

"It's going to have to," I say. I get dressed and leave as he protests and tries to convince me he was just joking. They are always "just joking"!

That night I add Channing Tatum to the list of people I follow on Instagram and remove Number Forty-Three. Channing won't disappoint me because we will never meet, and maybe men I will never meet are the best men to have crushes on right now.

Date Forty-Four: Exclamation Point!

To say that Number Forty-Four and I are dating would be a gross overstatement of our relationship. In fact, using the word "relationship" in context to Number Forty-Four is a gross overstatement of what it actually is, which is a few months filled with cybersex when his girlfriend is just out of earshot.

It didn't start out this way. It actually started out quite innocently, on Tinder. Ha! That statement about Tinder and innocence just made me laugh. Anyway, we matched, mutually expressed our disdain for the superficiality of online dating apps, and agreed that the best way for two people to see if they had chemistry was to just meet in person and immediately have sex.

And so we do.

And just to make sure we really and truly have chemistry, we have sex every week for an entire summer. I like him. I like him the first time I arrive at his doorstep wearing a fur coat and nothing else. I like him even more when he kisses me, and I like him the most when I log into Instagram one day and see that he has recently gotten himself a girlfriend. To his credit, the day he got his twenty-three-year-old, thin, blond, med-student, surfing girlfriend, he stops following me on Instagram and Snapchat and stops texting me.

His silence lasts for seven months. During those seven months, I pick up the super healthy habit of checking his Instagram once a day and watching his love story unfold before my very eyes. Number Forty-Four and Girlfriend hike, and surf, and brunch, and church. Number Forty-Four and Girlfriend hug and kiss and wear matching T-shirts—matching fucking T-shirts.

Then it is Valentine's Day, and Number Forty-Four is fed up with seven months of Girlfriend's sexual prudishness (I, for the record, am the very opposite of prudish, in case you haven't already guessed) and knows just who to complain about it to—me. While complaining, he reminisces about our various encounters—the carpet-burn incident, the open-window-while-neighbor-was-mowing-the-lawn debacle, and, my personal favorite, the ride-on-the-washing-machine encounter.

These walks down memory lane will (of course) lead to the inevitable sharing of nudes and, at the very least, a solo masturbation session for Number Forty-Four. This goes on for three months. Every time I see his name appear on my cell phone screen, I get a rush. Number Forty-Four wants me over Girlfriend. I am better than her. I am more desirable. I never pity her, even though I was once her, and my lack of empathy for her only makes me feel sorry for myself. Who am I becoming?

Number Forty-Four contacts me a few times a week for a virtual-amateur-porn-induced orgasm through Snapchat. Then he deletes me immediately so Girlfriend won't see my name on his phone. For three months, I give him unspoken permission to do this by way of my willing-ness to participate as his live-action, free-of-charge porn girl fantasy life. Not that I'm not getting anything out of it—I am. It is erotic most of the time (inconvenient at other times) and a huge boost to my crumbling ego, as I am going through a long stretch of particularly bad dates and good dates that keep ending with me being rejected.

Then on a Monday, I am coloring in my adult coloring book while listening to my favorite podcast. I have recently discovered that the combination of these two acts is comparable to sex and tequila in com-bating my anxiety and depression. While pausing to sharpen my sherbet-orange-colored pencil, I see a Snapchat alert pop up on my phone.

"Number Forty-Four has added you!"

Something about that exclamation point infuriates me. That little son-of-a-bitch punctuation mark is presumptuous enough to think I'm excited to have Number Forty-Four add me? No. Number Forty-Four should be excited that I *let* him add me! (Exclamation point!) I open Snapchat.

Number Forty-Four: Hey, babe. I'm thinking of you this morn-ing. Are you busy? I'm all alone.

And then, without hesitation or thought, as if my fingers are not parts of my body, they type out "Go away" with no period, no exclamation point, and definitely no question mark. "Go away" is all I type.

I delete Number Forty-Four, and then I block him from every social-media outlet I have, even the ones we are not friends on, so he can never find me.

I go back to coloring the French-pastry page in my Parisian coloring book.

Date Forty-Five: Exhale

The only thing I miss about small-town life is the sky," I say with longing. I am lying on the long green grass, surrounded by palm trees and stars that I cannot see because of the marine layer. Number Forty-Five is sitting on the cinder-block steps because he is afraid of spiders in the grass. He tries to blow the smoke from his lungs away from me, but the gray mass is drawn to my body like a magnet, like glitter— like men who will be moving soon.

He talks to me about the incomprehensible qualities of the physical sky and the infinite qualities of the universe and the never-ending war between religion and science, as I watch the smoke that had briefly lived inside his body dissipate into the blackness above me. He offers me the pipe. I inhale.

"Do you believe in God, or science?" he asks.

"Both," I say. The word leaves my lips so naturally—both. He's quiet. I continue without fear. "I believe both science and God exist, but I believe total faith in either of them is arrogant. To think that we humans can explain the world and the universe and God using words and Bibles and research is just so fucking arrogant." And even before I say the word "research," I know the relief that Number Nine was talking about in the backseat of that car sixteen months ago. Number Nine had felt relief in letting go of God, and I feel relief in letting go of my need to define God. God doesn't fit well into the boxes I've created for him my whole life, and he is free now—which, incidentally, is a horribly arrogant thing to say.

"If I bought you a ticket to Chicago, would you come?" he whispers in my ear as I exist in that space between awake and asleep. We are naked in his bed now—legs on torsos, arms on hands, skin on skin. Even though I don't remember how we got here, the trail of clothes I will find in the morning from the cinder-block stairs outside to the bedroom will be evidence that we didn't teleport as I had originally suspected in my semiconscious sleep state.

"Yes," I whisper back. "I always wanted to try deep-dish pizza."

"It's gross. You'll like the hot dogs better, but I'll take you to try some pizza if that's what you want."

Next thing I know, I'm almost dreaming again—about hot dogs, about pizza, about Chicago at Christmastime with Number Forty-Five. "I'm really going to miss you," he says with sincerity. "If I lived here any longer, I'd fall in love with you." And I believe him, not because it is true. It may or may not be true; I believe him simply because I am loveable.

I exhale and fall asleep.

Date Forty-Six: One Chocolate-Chip Pancake at a Time

As I descend the staircase in Lynnette's and my suburban home in my pajamas, I am relaxed. The house is clean. The pet rabbit is fed. The kids are gone. Lynnette is gone. I have the house to myself.

As I reach the last step, I notice a dry-erase whiteboard on an easel behind my gray-and-white paisley accent chair. The whiteboard has red writing all over it. The writing is large and small, in print and in cursive, and messy and neat. Some sentences are upside down; some words are vertical. All the words are for me.

I stand at the base of the easel, and it begins to expand through the roof. With each inch of its expansion, more words and sentences fill the white surface. The blue sky that comes in through the crack in the roof is like a flare, and the sunshine from outside is blinding, so I look straight ahead at the words that are in front of me.

My husband is next to me. He didn't appear next to me; he just simply is there, as if he had never left. He's wearing green. I can't see his face, but he's clean-shaven and smiling. Not in a happy way, really—just in a peaceful way. I savor the size of his body next to me. I'd forgotten what it felt like to be in his presence—to feel small and protected next to him. It was the way I felt that time he held me on a cot in the forest while we were camping.

We stand there, he and I, looking at the red words on the whiteboard. They are the words of every wrong he's ever done to me. They go on for infinity. They are phrases and words such as:

Forgetting your birthday but remembering hers

Cake

Shotgun

Buying her French fries while you were at the hospital

Blame

Telling her you were bad at blow jobs

Push

Bringing her into our kitchen

127

Videos

Suicide note

Verizon bill

Being inside her. Inside. *Her.*

Not mowing the lawn

Abandoning your children

Reading these while standing next to my husband makes me feel peaceful. To have all his transgressions in front of me, contained on a single whiteboard (even if that whiteboard stretches to infinite heights), brings me relief that the chaos is over now.

And I do want it to be over now.

And with this desire, a smooth, clean white rag appears in my left hand, even though I am right-handed.

With my husband's unspoken encouragement, I erase a single phrase. I don't know which of the phrases I erase because it doesn't matter. What matters is that I am the one who erases it.

My husband cannot erase what he's done. I have to—me.

There are so many more words to erase. So many phrases to eliminate, but today I will do one.

My husband reaches out to hold my left hand. The rag is gone. He leads me into the dining room like he once led me into the dining room of the cruise ship we were on for our honeymoon.

There is a couch in place of the dining room table, and we are lying on it. He's spooning me.

I feel the slow rise and fall of his chest into my back.

His breath makes contact with the skin on my neck—the skin only his breath can reach because of the way his body fits into mine. I close my eyes and exhale—pleasure.

Then, there's a fart, a fart so loud that it wakes me from my dream. It's a fart only a mother could love, a fart from one of my kids. Somewhere within all the madness, tenderness for my children had not only returned, but it had increased.

I realize this, just now. Good morning to me.

The sensations from my dream are still vivid, my emotions raw. I want to cry in relief. Finally, after more than two years of night terrors, I have a peace-filled dream about my husband, and I can feel that this dream is the faint budding of the hope that was taken from me so long ago.

The gentle stirring of my daughter is a reminder that I cannot cry. I have children who need me to be intact, children who both crawled into my bed last night after mutual nightmares about corpses. We go through the morning-after-a-nightmare question ritual.

"What feelings were you having in your dream?"

"Why do you think you're having those feelings?"

"Is there a way I can help you express those feelings during the day so they don't get stuck in your brain and come out while you're sleeping?"

In the midst of this, Number Forty-Six texts me his usual "Good morning" text, and I ask him to take me out tonight. I need to get away. My children's suffering makes me want to run away to a man. *My* suffering makes me want to run away to a man. Sometimes just waking up makes me want to run away to a man.

"Who wants to go on a breakfast date with Mommy?" I say after setting up a date with Number Forty-Six. The kids and I go to IHOP—the three musketeers working through their grief, one chocolate-chip pancake at a time.

Later that night, I go on my date with Number Forty-Six.

I guess this is the part of my story where I should write about how I got better, about how my peaceful dream was a turning point. I should tell a story about how I fell in love with Number Forty-Six (a man whom I met in the produce section of a grocery store) and how this love healed my broken heart and erased my bitterness.

I should write about how I found a counselor, got on medications for my anxiety and depression, and devoted my life to God and suicide-awareness charities. I should write about how I traveled once a month and exercised and wrote in journals. I should write about how I meditated in a damn forest.

But I never wanted to write a book like that. And even if I did, none of those things actually happened to me. First of all, my date with Number Forty-Six (a man I actually met in a dive bar) ended with us having sex on a dirty brown pullout couch, followed by him asking me to be in a threesome with him and his roommate. Second of all, I have never found healing in conventional ways such as counseling sessions and philanthropy, and I wouldn't be caught dead meditating in a damn forest.

I know a lot of people have found healing in these ways, and I have heard their stories and read their books—retrospective ones told several years or decades after a divorce or a death. Their stories are profound, thought provoking, neat, tidy, and oh so very healthy. Their stories are not mine. Not yet.

I wanted to tell stories about grief in its infancy and the mess of it all.

I wanted to tell stories about the growth and epiphanies I found in the unhealthy choices I made before the healthy ones became my only options.

I wanted to tell stories about the unfair, selfish blame and rage I directed at my husband for his suicide and chronic adultery, instead of acknowledging both acts as a symptom of mental illness.

I wanted to tell stories that might provoke me one day to consider the possibility of forgiveness. Forgiveness of my husband for being sick, and stubborn, and selfish. Forgiveness of the other women for being lonely, and pretty, and broken. Forgiveness of myself for being all of these things and more.

I wanted to tell stories about how for some of us, accepting our losses means merely having the desire to heal because just wanting to heal is all the bravery we can muster for now.

And more than anything, I wanted to tell stories about how the depths of our grief are directly proportionate to the amount of love we had for the things and people that were taken from us.

And I loved my husband, John.

Acknowledgments and Answering the Question:

Aren't You Worried Your Children

Will Read This Book One Day?

This is not the book I wanted to publish. The original manuscript for *Boys, Booze, and Bathroom Floors* was double the size and far more salacious. When I originally began writing my story in 2014, I did so from a place of vengeance and rage. At the time, this outlet was helpful and necessary. I do not regret penning it, but I would have regretted its publication.

The first version of this manuscript went into the dirty marital details that the general population would have loved to read: shocking betrayals, hospitalizations, STI tests, physical altercations, eating disorders, antidepressants, stalking of the other women, and enough sex tapes to put the Kardashian clan to shame. In the end though, facing the legal ramifications of such a story, and more importantly facing the possibility of my children one day seeing their father represented in such a way, caused me to rethink this project.

That was in December of 2015.

I spent the next few months mulling over the decision of whether or not to move on with publishing my story. I was prepared to defend myself against possible lawsuits, but was I prepared to one day explain to my children why, in the wake of their father's suicide, I felt the need to publish a book that showcased him as the villain? Was it okay to use my art for catharsis when it had the possibility of damaging my kids?

The answer was no. I am first a mother, and then a writer.

Still though, I had promised myself a published book by the end of 2016, and damn it I was going to do it! It was from there, I was forced to test the limits of my creativity and the current version of this book was conceived. I had to write about my life experience in a way that was truthful about my anger, therapeutic for my sadness, and entertaining to my audience all while being respectful to the memory of my late husband for my children's sake. I had to write a story with all the compelling elements of cheating, sex, emotional outbursts, and nervous breakdowns without throwing my deceased husband under the bus; and so, I threw myself.

I chose to write more about my reactions to the things done to me instead of the details of what was done and who did them. I took responsibility for the way in which I grieved, exposing all the undesirable parts about myself. I faced the humbling fact that I am no better than my husband; I too am sick, and selfish, and broken....we all are.

But we are more than just the bad choices we make. We are more than just the dark sides of our innate personalities. We are all beautiful, and tender, and benevolent-even my late husband who hurt me so deeply that I became a different person. This epiphany gave me the ability to forgive myself and to see that while I was someone who had been victimized, I had the choice of whether or not to *be* that victim.

Some days I still choose victimhood, but most days I refute it.

Should my children ever read my memoir (although I doubt they will be eager to read a story about their mother's grief-fueled sex life), I am confident that the ways in which their father and I have been represented in this book combined with their real life memories of us, will give them the best gift I believe I have to offer as a parent. I have presented to them an honest and accurate portrayal of who John and I really were and are; the good, the bad, and the very, very ugly. I believe once a child is presented with their guardian's flaws in a way that is without shame, it gives them permission to be forthright and unashamed of their own flaws as a developing human, which leads to love, acceptance, and a greater understanding for themselves and the human condition.

Thank you everyone for your kind words and support throughout this process. There are too many of you to individually name, and for that I am grateful and humbled. This has been a very difficult and terrifying process for me. Had it not been for all of my online and in-life supporters, I would've given up my life-long dream of publishing a book; thank you for not allowing me to do so.

Thank you especially to "Lynnette," who has physically and willingly lived through this with me. Thank you to Lisa who has never allowed distance to diminish her commitment to our best-friendship. Thank you to my sisters, April, Tina, Kina, and Alexis who love me without condition. Thank you to Allyssa for giving me a safe, non-judgmental place to fall. Thank you to Paul Ribera and Jenny Jaramillo Chayes for making my book cover a piece of art. Thank you to Vee Nelson, my solo cheerleader, whose music validates me. Thank you to Robert who has simply been there since I was eight years old. And thank you to my parents who always bought me pencils, paper, churros, and blankets. I love you all more than I love chocolate cake!

If You Want to Stalk Me

Michelle is a beach-living, child-raising, Nutella-eating, book-writing, social media–addicted suicide widow living with her best friend, five children, and a bunny in San Diego, California. You can follow her continued grief process, dating disasters, and current and future writing projects here:

Twitter: @mouthy_michelle

Instagram: @mouthy_michelle

Made in the USA
San Bernardino, CA
14 February 2018